The Treasure of the Parables

The Treasure

of the

Parables

by MSGR. LUCIEN CERFAUX

Translated by M. BENT

ST. NORBERT ABBEY PRESS
De Pere, Wisconsin
U. S. A.
1968

Excerpts from *The Jerusalem Bible,* copyright © 1966 by **Darton,** Longman & Todd, Ltd. and Doubleday and Company, Inc. Used by permission of the publishers.

Edited by Lisa McGaw

Originally published as *Le Trésor des Paraboles* by Editions Charles Desclee et Cie, Tournai, Belgium

© 1968 St. Norbert Abbey Press

Standard Book Number 8316-1026-3
Library of Congress Catalog Card Number 68-58123

Printed in the United States of America
ST. NORBERT ABBEY PRESS
De Pere, Wisconsin 54115

CONTENTS

PROLOGUE   1

PART ONE: THE MYSTERIES OF THE
   KINGDOM OF GOD   13
     I. The Sowing of the Kingdom   20
    II. The Antithesis of the Kingdom   43
   III. The Encounter with the Kingdom   56

PART TWO: THE NEW JUSTICE   65
    IV. The Mercy of God   66
     V. The Just According to the Heart of God   72
    VI. The Break   92

PART THREE: THE ETERNAL HARVEST   107
   VII. The Judgment of God   109
  VIII. The Coming in Glory of Jesus   121
EPILOGUE   139

The man who first conceived of writing began by drawing or painting houses, trees, and birds. He wrote as he thought, in images. The East has preserved for us its ancient pictographic writings, and familiarizes us still in our own day with images that delighted the "imaginations" of a less intellectual humanity. The "parable" is of the nature of the image or picture. The Greeks defined it in their rhetoric as the juxtaposition, to an idea less immediately accessible, from an analogy concrete enough to clarify the abstract idea. It is thus today that the master teaches his disciples, or how, during a lecture, we attempt to revive attention.

Among the Semites, the parable is encased in the "image" and possesses a quite particular richness of suggestion. For them one term serves to designate all that we call parable, proverb, fable, comparison, allegory, or metaphor. In all these they again find the "image" concept of the primitive language. Where we think in "ideas," they think in "images." The image is like the fulcrum and the launching pad of their intelligence. It is also a symbol to "decipher." Within the image is already visible, to a variable degree, the "cipher" that leads to a knowledge envisioned from the beginning. The great art is to hide the final objective sufficiently: to hide it and reveal it at the same time. When the cipher or the key is inaccessible to the uninitiated, image becomes enigma —thus, what Samson proposed to the Philistines: "Out of the eater came what is eaten,/ and out of the strong came what is sweet" (Judg. 14:14). On the other hand, we comprehend without difficulty what Nathan is driving at when he contrives his anecdote and recounts it to David: "In the same town were two men, one rich, the other poor. . . . The poor man had nothing but a ewe lamb. . . ." A traveler, having arrived at the home of the rich man, steals the poor man's sheep. David, caught in the trap, condemns the rich man. "You," says the prophet, "are the [rich] man." Moreover, the prophet had strongly stressed the tenderness of the poor man for his only sheep. That was the key (cf. 2 Sam. 12:1-15).

Sometimes the cipher is so obvious that one could not fail to perceive it upon first seeing the "image." Such is allegory: image and signification mixed in one narration, one description. The mixture can attain to the refined art of the prophet Isaiah in his "song of the vineyard." The listeners knew that Israel was the vineyard of God, but Isaiah paints this with such realism that his listeners have only the wine country of the hills before their eyes:

> My friend had a vineyard
> on a fertile hillside.

The winegrower deals harshly with his unprofitable vineyard and in the end cries out:

> I will command the clouds
> to rain no rain on it.

The veil of the allegory is rent. Everyone understood
him:

> Yes, the vineyard of Yahweh Sabaoth,
> is the House of Israel (Isa. 5:1-7).

However, one cannot distinguish so strongly between the Greek parable and the Semitic "image"
so as to dig an impassable moat between them. Can
one compare two things without an interplay of
mutual reactions being established between them?
Moreover, especially in the days of the evangelists,
the ancient civilizations of Greece and the East over-
lapped in a thousand ways: in art, literature, politics,
and religion.

Thus Jesus also made use of the Greek parable.
To oblige him, as A. Jülicher and his current disciples
maintain, to make use of this only, to the exclusion
of the Semitic "image" in its allegorical form, is a
mere speculation which is denounced both by historical credibilities and by careful exegesis of these
parables, all of which are steeped in the Semitic
milieu. For no Gospel parable is crystal clear, and
explanations are not superfluous.

T. W. Manson points out that the Synoptic parables cannot all comply with Jülicher's hypothesis;
for example, the parable: "Nothing that goes into a
man from outside can make him unclean; it is the
things that come out of a man that make him unclean"
(Mark 7:15) is enigmatic. The theory would lead us,
he continues, to reject the authenticity of passages
such as Mark 4:11f. If one renounces this radical

treatment of Gospel material, it is necessary to revise the definition of a parable, a process which leads us to the beginning of an inquiry according to the rhetoric of the Old Testament, rather than according to the "rhetoricians" of the West. This is precisely what we are going to do.

Could God speak to us otherwise than in "images"? It is in "signs" that he revealed himself to the "seers" and to the "divines" of the past. The prophetic visions are "images." In this manner he proclaimed the destiny of Israel to the prophet Amos:

> This is what the Lord Yahweh showed me:
> a basket of ripe fruit:
> "What do you see, Amos?" he asked.
> "A basket of ripe fruit," I said.
> Then Yahweh said,
> "My people Israel is ripe for destruction."
>
> Amos 8:1-2

Amos had looked at baskets of ripe fruit a hundred times. But that day he noticed that particular basket as if he had never seen one before. He knew instinctively that God wanted him to regard it, and that it was going to signify something: one of those secrets which God communicates to his servants, the prophets. The prophet's understanding had been guided by God in order that he might discover, beneath an "image," a more profound reality.

God will make use of this revelatory process throughout the Old Testament. An image which suddenly appears in a religious light—a dream, a story, the encounter with an unexpected sight—instantly stirs up an as yet vague intellectual illumination. From this intuition, divine thought is clarified for man.

Let us recall several stages in this long history. We know of the matrimonial adventures of Hosea. The prophet attributes to his marriage—real or fictitious—with Gomer, daughter of Diblaim, a symbolic significance which is revealed to him step by step (in order to foresee Israel's future) in the explanation of the names imposed by God upon the children of this unhappy union (Hos. 1:2-2:3).

The vision of the plague of locusts, in the beginning of the book of Joel, serves to support a description (framed in a liturgy of mourning and supplication) of the terrors of the Day of Yahweh. Isaiah's song of the vineyard, another stage, leads us to Ezekiel and his well-known allegory of the eagle, the cedar, and the vine (ch. 17). There the revelation theme could not be more clear:

The word of Yahweh was addressed to me as follows, "Son of man, ask them a riddle; propound a parable to the House of Israel. Say, 'The Lord Yahweh says this:

> A large eagle, with huge wings
> and a wide span,
> covered with speckled feathers,
> came to Lebanon.
> He took hold of the top of the cedar,
> plucked off the top branch,
> carried it off to the land of merchants.' "

One quickly recalls Nebuchadnezzar and his expeditions. The branch becomes an ever more opulent vine. We should not be surprised to see a cedar branch produce a vine, for this is the vine of Isaiah and of the entire prophetic tradition. The allegory is carried on, becoming more and more complicated, until an explanation is thrust upon us:

The word of Yahweh was addressed to me as follows:

"Say to that set of rebels, 'Do you not know what this means?' Say this, 'Listen; the king of Babylon came to Jerusalem, . . .' "

On the same note, and drawing the allegory to a close, God renews his messianic promises, which need no explanation:

> From the top of the cedar,
> from the highest branch I will take a shoot
> and plant it myself on a very high mountain.
> I will plant it on the high mountain of Israel.
> It will sprout branches and bear fruit,
> and become a noble cedar.
> Every kind of bird will live beneath it,
> every winged creature rest in the shade of
>   its branches.
> And every tree of the field will learn that I,
>   Yahweh, am the one
> who stunts tall trees and makes the low ones
>   grow, . . .

Nebuchadnezzar leads us to the book of Daniel,

and this furnishes us with a last stop, on the threshold
of the apocalyptic period. The dreams of Nebuchadnezzar—dreams are of the family of symbols—mysteriously reveal the future. In order to understand their
meaning, the king in vain summons his sages; on the
other hand, Daniel, the Hebrew child, receives the
meaning of the visions through revelation, and declares to the king: "There is a God in heaven who
reveals mysteries, and who has shown King Nebuchadnezzar what is to take place in the days to come"
(Dan. 2:28). At this point we hear the word "mystery"
for the first time: a prelude to the revelation of the
secrets of the Kingdom in the New Testament.

The themes encountered in the Old Testament are
retained in Jesus' teaching, particularly utilization of
the parable as a method of revelation. The Master
of Galilee was the heir of the prophets. Moreover,
the relationship between his parables and those of
Amos or Isaiah does not detract at all from their
original and artistic character. The originality of the
ancients did not consist in denying the tradition of
previous masters, but in following in their tracks.
Amos and Isaiah were great poets. Though recalling
their art, even imitating it, the poetry of Jesus loses
nothing of its spontaneity and freshness. His parables,
wrote C. H. Dodd, have an imaginative and poetic
quality: they are works of art. But one did not count
poets by the thousands in that small human society
which was Palestine at the beginning of our era.
Neither the monks of Qumran nor the Pharisees
possessed, to our knowledge, this understanding of

nature which makes poets. No more so did the evangelists possess it: neither Mark, an excellent storyteller, nor Luke, who knew how to write, were poets. The fishermen on Lake Genesareth, or the tax collectors, or the simple Galilean women had no more reason to be familiar with this aristocratic art. Does not the splendor of religious feeling which the parables reveal—that profound and crystalline religious thought belonging to Jesus, with the freshness of his poetry—suffice to mark him, among his contemporaries, as a unique genius?

We speak much of life according to "tradition" in the Christian community at a time when "written tradition" was not yet completely fixed. Do we remember more precisely that the role of "tradition" is not to "create" memories, but to preserve them? Would the Christian community have attributed to Jesus the parables gathered together in its midst, rather than to repeat indefinitely the artistic creations with which he had enriched its treasury? One of those best acquainted with Christian origins and with Judaism, J. Jeremias, has justly written: "The parables are a fragment of the rock on which tradition is built. In effect, it is generally admitted that images [pictures] are more deeply imprinted upon the memory than any abstract idea. And when it is a question of the parables of Jesus, one must add that they reflect faithfully and with a particular distinctness the 'Good News' which he announces, the eschatological character of his preaching, the earnestness of his calls to repentance and his conflicts with Pharisaism. On the other hand, underlying the Greek text is to be seen everywhere the maternal language of Jesus, and it is from daily life in Palestine that the very matter of his images is borrowed."

Our first concern will be to hear the authentic voice of Jesus. This is the work of the exegete. That voice alone is truly efficient.

From two diametrically opposed poles, Dodd and Claudel express in approximately the same manner the efficacy of the parables. No exegetical pedantry, declares Dodd, can prevent those—who, according to Jesus' expression have "the ears to hear"—from experiencing that the parables "apply to their own state in life."

Paul Claudel gives these words to Christ: "The miracles were signs, but figures of speech and parables are also signs, schematic events confronting the spirit, not a means for possessing me, but for following me; to follow that which, passing through the midst of you, will go further on." For him, all is parable and symbolizing image in the Bible. "A lion, a cedar, an eagle," he explains, "we know what these are; and when someone names them in our presence, there is something within us which adapts itself, which fashions itself in their likeness, which takes their form and their color, which attaches itself to their being. In like manner when we are told of the prodigal son or the story of Absalom, we become in turn the father and the vagabond, the old king and his stabbed son. We become Elijah and the Samaritan and the villainous Heliodorus, flogged by the angels, and the four-legged Nebuchadnezzar—even the five-legged one which we can admire in the Louvre. Our entire being is transformed into someone who listens and sees. All our faculties are suspended in favor of attention and imagination. The clever writer, for a moment, makes us become what he wishes."

Let us pass over literature. Indeed, each true and great work of art speaks directly to our souls and raises them to the ideal of the artist. But when the artist is at the same time the revealer of God's mysteries, literature becomes revelation itself. The Gospel parables represent divine realities. Chosen knowingly by Our Lord, they carry in themselves even today the thought and the life of the divine artist. Indeed, they are compelling in any language and in all literature, but it is the divine Word that pronounced them. It is he who will assure them resemblance with the divine original toward which they impel us. Our Lord does not abandon them. When we meditate upon them, his grace—present at the same time within us—imprints the images upon us, and identifies us with them.

This is why the exegete strives to attain to the word of Christ as it was presented to us in a moment of history, in a province of Palestine, among the Jewish people with their temporal, geographic and political conjectures, and all the heritage of an eventful religious past. It is through all this veneer, scarcely a veil, that the profound voice of the revelation of God's Son—who willed himself to be man

before being Jew—will become intensified in order
to strike our hearts, revealing in them a connaturality
with the divine creation sleeping within us which we
will have to state precisely if we truly wish to interpret the Master's intentions. Along with Jesus' voice
we will also hear that of Catholic tradition: this is
our right and our duty.

We will concern ourselves with three groups of
parables, which are, moreover, those that Christian
people most readily reread. The layout of our work
is thus constituted, successively perusing the parables of the Kingdom, those of the new justice, and
those which help us cross the threshold of eternity.

PART ONE

THE MYSTERIES OF THE KINGDOM OF GOD

We approach at the outset the most original section of the Gospel parables, the third great "discourse" of Matthew's Gospel, presented also in Mark and in Luke. Matthew begins with the parable of the sower and its explanation, separated by logia, gathering together, as we like to say today, **ipsissima verba** of Christ. Parables follow which are normally introduced by the formula: "The kingdom of heaven (or of God) may be compared to . . . ."

These parables, in fact, define the actual foundation of the Kingdom of heaven under various aspects. As a whole they present the lesson drawn by Jesus from the experience of his activity in Galilee and constitute one of the most authentic portions of his teaching. A primitive Gospel document already contained the substance of it. First we must again present the circumstances which led Jesus to pass from the announcement of the good news of the Kingdom of heaven, and from the proclamation of the dispositions which it requires, to the explanation of the "mystery" of the divine plan establishing the Kingdom foretold by the prophets.

In Galilee, Jesus accomplished the program laid

out by the prophet Isaiah. Over a period of months,
he announced "the good news of the kingdom of
God." He knew himself to be the messenger of whom
Isaiah had written:

> How beautiful on the mountains,
> are the feet of one who brings good news,
> who heralds peace, brings happiness,
> proclaims salvation,
> and tells Zion,
> "Your God is king!"
>
> Listen! Your watchman raise their voices,
> they shout for joy together,
> for they see Yahweh face to face,
> as he returns to Zion.
>
> Isaiah 52:7-8

However, the achievement which his message at
the same time announced and fulfilled exceeded the
descriptions of the Old Testament prophet in religious value. Isaiah could neither totally free himself from a nationalistic dream nor wipe out the too
human colors which shrouded the authentic work of
God. And it was this dream and these colors above
all which held Christ's contemporaries spellbound.
For Jesus, the "peace" which he proclaimed was entirely within, and the miraculous "happiness," which
was partly present, was only the covering for a
spiritual reality. It is in this sense that he replied to
the doubts of the Baptist and his messengers: ". . . the
blind see again, and the lame walk, lepers are
cleansed, and the deaf hear, and the dead are raised

to life and the Good News is proclaimed to the poor;
and happy is the man who does not lose faith in me"
(Matt. 11:5; cf. Luke 7:22).

Such a message was too far above the hopes of
the common people. The messenger of the Kingdom
brought to life again the rebuff of former prophets,
which Isaiah had depicted in a celebrated passage in
Jewish tradition:

> You will listen and listen again, but not
> understand,
> see and see again, but not perceive.
> For the heart of this nation has grown coarse,
> their ears are dull of hearing, and they have
> shut their eyes,
> for fear they should see with their eyes,
> hear with their ears,
> understand with their heart,
> and be converted
> and be healed by me.
> Isaiah 6:9-10, as cited in Matthew 13:14-15

Isaiah added some threats, including with them
the implicit promise of a better future:

> [The country] will be stripped like a terebinth
> of which, once felled, only the stock remains.
> The stock is a holy seed.
>
> Isaiah 6:13

He spoke in the light of a "remnant":

> Those who are left of Zion
> and remain of Jerusalem

shall be called holy
and those left in Jerusalem, noted down
for survival.
Isaiah 4:3

This "holy remnant" Jesus saw being born under his eyes within the limited group of his faithful disciples, the little flock to whom the Kingdom had been given (Luke 12:32).

Isaiah and the prophets of old said simply, "God reigns," using the verb when they spoke of the intervention of God as prepared to govern directly, in person, his chosen people. The formula which Jesus employs, "kingdom of heaven" (Matt.), suggests that the Kingdom is at the same time both celestial and earthly, and that the God of heaven is its king. This is the atmosphere of the book of Daniel.

And sovereignty and kingship,
and the splendours of all the kingdoms
under heaven
will be given to the people of the saints
of the Most High.
His sovereignty is an eternal sovereignty
and every empire will serve and obey him.
Daniel 7:27

But going beyond Daniel's idea, the Kingdom of God, for Jesus, remains essentially "spiritual." Daniel will furnish only the schematics which Jesus uses to "reveal" the basis of his doctrine; that is to say, the mysterious plan of God—in particular this word "mystery," to which correspond "revelation" and "initiates." To Daniel's formula: "There is a God in heaven who reveals mysteries . . ." (Dan. 2:28), the Gospel logion replies: "The mysteries of the kingdom of heaven are revealed to you . . ." (Matt. 13:11).

Daniel distinguishes between those who receive the revelation (the "children" of the Book) and the sages of Babylon (regarding the meaning of Nebuchadnezzar's dream): "None of the sages, enchanters, magicians or wizards has been able to tell the king the truth of the mystery which the king propounded, but there is a God in heaven who reveals mysteries, and who has shown King Nebuchadnezzar what is to take place in the days to come" (Dan. 2:27-28).[1] Jesus will say in a solemn "benediction": "I bless you, Father, Lord of heaven and of earth, for hiding these things 'from the learned and the clever' (cf. Dan. 1:20) and revealing them to mere children" (Matt. 11:25). Again he will say, in that form of "beatitude" familiar to him, when addressing his privileged disciples: "But happy are your eyes because they see, your ears because they hear! I tell you solemnly, many prophets and holy men longed to see what you see, and never saw it; to hear what you hear, and never heard it" (Matt. 13:11, 13, 16-17).

The mystery of the Kingdom consists of a paradox. One waits for a feat of strength from God, and one finds oneself facing a secret intervention, stirred up in the depths of souls by the "Good News" of Jesus, and practically restricted to the "poor." But a future is promised for this humble beginning. Now, this contrast between the "littleness" of the beginning

and the "greatness" of the final success of the
Kingdom of God is expressed by Ezekiel and Daniel
within the context of "parables." The cedar branch
becomes an opulent vine (Ezek. 17:1-8) or else a
noble cedar (Ezek. 17:22-23); the stone broken away
from the mountain grew into a great mountain, filling
the whole earth (Nebuchadnezzar's dream, Dan. 2:35).
Certain textual similarities clearly establish the de-
pendence of the parable of the mustard seed becoming a great tree upon these passages of the Old
Testament.

Thus in this way the prophets furnished Jesus
with the formulas and images with which he dressed
his thought, and even the parabolic, literary genre
that helped him to continue, in spite of the turmoil
in Galilee, to proclaim the Good News—with the hope
of attainment for those capable of hearing—and at the
same time to reveal the mystery of the Kingdom of
God to his disciples. He "would speak in parables."
The people would continue to listen, to marvel,
perhaps to come back to him; to his disciples he
would explain the hidden meaning of these images,
carrying with them the revelation of God. He would
reveal to them the mysterious design which presided
over the founding of the Kingdom: "The mysteries of
the kingdom of heaven are revealed to you."

Only a Master like Jesus had the necessary
authority to introduce within Judaism a doctrine so
flagrantly novel.

The Kingdom, as Daniel spoke of it, is the little
stone detached from the mountain, falling from

heaven solely through divine will and destined to become, on earth, a mountain which will cover it, ascending anew toward heaven. The beginning of the eschatological manifestation (the fullness of time arrived among us) is in Christ's message and in that of the apostles. Their word, that which goes forth from the mouth of God and does not return to him empty (Isa. 55:10-11), is the seed which makes ready the divine harvest.

[1]The French biblical quotation reads: ". . . at the end of time."

THE SOWING
OF THE KINGDOM

Of the two symbols for the establishment of the Kingdom on earth, the sowing and the harvest, the Old Testament gives greater weight to the latter. God is the harvester of eternity who intervenes finally at the end of time. He is the grape-picker. His "day" is a joy for the elect, but it is also a day of wrath on which, amid fire, its "judge" is manifested to the world.

At first, Jesus picked up the symbol of the harvest. His apostles had been sent to reap: "The harvest is rich but the labourers are few, so ask the Lord of the harvest to send labourers to his harvest" (Matt. 9:37-38; Luke 10:2). But one reaps only after having sown; and the joy of the harvest dries the tears of planting time. The Kingdom of God, in order to be a crop, will first be a seed.

The Sower (Matt. 13:1-9; Mark 4:3-9; Luke 8:4-8)

The setting of the Synoptics evokes a familiar picture: the Lake of Capernaum, motionless in the elongated oval of its hills; a fishing bark in which Christ is seated, surrounded by his disciples, the crowd on the shore. Dare we risk overloading the picture by adding a sower somewhere on a furrowed slope in the background? The farmer is conscious of his task: he is sowing his children's bread, that bread which fortifies bodies.

". . . Imagine a sower going out to sow. As he sowed, some seeds fell on the edge of the path, and the birds came and ate them up. Others fell on patches of rock where they found little soil and sprang up straight away, because there was no depth of earth; but as soon as the sun came up they were scorched and, not having any roots, they withered away. Others fell among thorns, and the thorns grew up and choked them. Others fell on rich soil and produced their crop, some a hundredfold, some sixty, some thirty. Listen, anyone who has ears!" (Matt. 13:4-9).

Jesus' gaze, rising again to heaven, prolongs the earthly scene. There is a planting other than the temporal planting, infinitely more precious and more important. God's world also has crops which grow for him. Jesus contemplates these. It is God who has done the essential work. He is "the Sower."

The sowing of the Kingdom had been the first thing willed, the first created. The planting done by the Galilean farmer is its image. He does not work fields like our fields, those abundant plains where wheat undulates in the wind and turns slowly yellow beneath sun and rain, but fields of countries scorched by the sun, unprofitable land. Paths cross fields without well-defined boundaries, seeds fall, and the sparrows are ravenous. The cultivable soil has little depth, and limestone abounds.

A parable, according to certain exegetes, cannot jump the fence which separates it from allegory. But if Jesus related in detail the layout of the field, and if he did this while thinking of the partial failure of his mission in Galilee, why did not the terrain's restrictions explain the causes of his failure? According to God's thought, land turned toward the midday sun; today we realize that it inclines toward the north. "[The land] shall yield you brambles and thistles" (Gen. 3:18). The disappointments of planters are proverbial. "Wheat they have sown, thorns they reap" (Jer. 12:13). Planting is done in tears. One could say that autumn itself, the planting season, touches on melancholy. "It was an autumn day, sad and cold. The Sower went out to plant . . ." (Joergensen, **The Parables**). The farmer, in those ancient times when famines were not rare, took his sack of seed in advance from the food provision necessary for his family; and he depended neither on the good will of the sky—with its bad winters and its droughts —nor on being spared by bands of nomads or the passing-through of armed troops.

Each year the laborer again begins the planting of his land. Jesus, the divine Sower, has not ceased from generation to generation his work in Galilee. The renewal of the Church promises us young and fertile wheatfields; yet first we must listen. "Hear, anyone who has ears!" Let us reread our parable, thinking of today's planting.

A portion of the seed falls along the way, and the birds are ravenous. Even if the seed touches the soil, the land is hard, unable to receive the seed. All generations are the same. Ours is neither better nor worse than others. But today we openly banish God. We are the road; we wish to be; and we do everything to harden it, to macadamize it. Happily, faith assures us that this hardness is a pose, a covering which cracks as soon as circumstances oblige man to descend within himself and to perceive that he is not God.

A portion of the seed falls upon patches of rock. The earthbed is shallow. The seed sprouts at once, thanks to the moisture of a rain or of the night dew; but when the sun rises and darts down its rays, the sprout withers.

All goes well. We are afire with the idealistic causes which our times multiply—for any moment at all. Life clears up this deception, because God takes pleasure only in solid things. "Should some trial come, or some persecution on account of the word, they fall away at once" (Mark 4:17). Courageous men begin again.

A portion of the seed falls among thorns. One encounters excellent men on the way, those whom one would dream of making workers for the Kingdom. But there are thorns: love of gain, of pleasure; the anxiety of the age; the illusions of riches—all explain the parable. The seed is choked, and still worse, men use the soil of religion to obtain a better luxuriance of thorns.

Finally, there remains the **good** soil, that which

produces thirty, sixty, and a hundredfold. It is said that fiftyfold is maximum production in the best land, but the parable places itself above statistics. "Isaac sowed his crops in that land [the land of Gerar], and that year he reaped a hundred fold" (Gen. 26:12). Such a harvest was exceptional even for the patriarch. The saints are the hundredfold crop.

God's power is vindicated by the attainments of the good soil. And this is the point of the parable. In spite of the obstacles (St. Paul would say: Because of the obstacles) God's power is at work, and it succeeds where man fails.

The apparent failures of Jesus did not shake his confidence in God: they were accounted for in the revelation of the mystery of the Kingdom, which is God's power within weakness.

Jesus' disciples, the Twelve at first, were to retain the lesson. Throughout their failures and persecutions, they will accomplish their task; they will sow, they will plant the Church. To the Christians after them, those charged with the ministry or the simple faithful, will be proved true the mysterious law which regulates, from the time of planting, the progress of the crops. God wishes to rely upon the terrains he created. His second creation does not utterly renew the first; his grace acts upon a primary stock, deteriorated by sin. It is from this perspective that he asks for and accepts our collaboration, and asks us to be that good soil, moist and warm, which splits open the seed and makes it grow out of its own substance in order that the seed and the earth make but one entity.

Let us listen, therefore, to Augustine the bishop, the great theologian and scriptural scholar, as he explains and applies the parable to his priests and faithful: "Change while it is possible; till the hard areas with the plow again; throw the rocks out of the field; uproot the thorns. Harden not the heart; this will cause the word of God to die immediately. Have not shallow soil where charity cannot deeply take root. Do not permit the cares and desires of the age to choke the good seed, which our labors pour out upon you. But be the good earth. . . . One yields a hundredfold, another sixty, another thirtyfold; the fruits are more or less great in each. But all will be brought to the granery."

Such is our consolation and our joy. God's granery is vast, and his grace is doubtless larger than anything we can imagine. It possesses resources, and it knows how to use stratagems which his mercy devises minute by minute until the end of all human life. The parable makes us reflect upon human weakness, in order that God's mercy and our confidence may grow unhampered.

The Darnel in the Wheatfield (Matt. 13:24-30)

Another parable adds to the vicissitudes of planting.

"The kingdom of heaven may be compared to a man who sowed good seed in his field. While everybody was asleep his enemy came, sowed darnel all among the wheat, and made off. When the new wheat sprouted and ripened, the darnel appeared as well. The owner's servants went to him and said, 'Sir, was it not good seed that you sowed in your field? If so, where does the darnel come from?' 'Some enemy has done this' he answered. And the servants said, 'Do you want us to go and weed it out?' But he said, 'No, because when you weed out the darnel you might pull up the wheat with it. Let them both grow till the harvest; and at harvest time I shall say to the reapers: First collect the darnel and tie it in bundles to be burnt, then gather the wheat into my barn.'"

Exegetes familiar with the Holy Land provide some valuable bits of information.

"Wheat, ordinarily attaining to a more consider-able height than darnel, the farmers, with their sickles, cut the wheat above the darnel so that the darnel spikes are not touched. During that process one often hears the overseer say to the reapers: Raise your hands higher" (Biever, priest of the Latin Patriarchate of Jerusalem).

"In the villages of Palestine it is common that a man has his particular enemy, and agricultural venge-ance is very frequent: trees cut down, crops burned" (Lagrange).

"To avert the faithful from these dreadful venge-ances, the crime of cutting down a fruit tree is a reserved sin in the diocese of Jerusalem" (Buzy).

"It is possible that the parable of the darnel

recalls a real incident, since we have been told a similar story in modern Palestine. . . . This is the custom . . . . To extirpate the darnel, and even several times . . ." (J. Jeremias).

The explanation of the parable preserved by Matthew is strongly allegorical: "The field is the world. The servants are man. The harvesters are the angels." St. Jerome improves upon this: ". . . the men who sleep (when they should have kept watch) are the doctors of the churches." Exegetes go to excesses of this kind in order to bring the parable back to a simple pronouncement from which Jesus draws a lesson in patience while waiting for the judgment of God.

Indeed, the Master of Galilee had to vindicate his actions and his method for bringing about the Kingdom in the face of contemporary prejudices. The precursor himself, the Zealots, the Pharisees, the anchorites of Qumran were in accord, demanding stringent measures from God: a spectacular intervention for the establishment of the Kingdom. Around Jesus a band of disciples and sympathizers came and went; Galilean men and women continued their daily life. Jesus did not interfere. He did not even stop the evil on the threshold of his little community. But truly, would he have wished to give a banal lesson in patience?

Matthew, and before him an Aramaic source, placed our parable in the over-all context of the revelation of the mystery of the Kingdom. This is an indication that the question here concerns the polity of God and the plan for the founding of the Kingdom —which carries with it a certain type of allegory. The farmer represents God, and the field is his Kingdom; behind the enemy is hidden something or someone, that Power of Evil in the depths of man— sometimes nameless, sometimes under a very personal aspect—and which thwarts God's work; and the fire that will burn the bundles of darnel has a somewhat eschatological odor, like the fiery furnace in the book of Daniel. Galilee was that portion of the immense field where God began the planting of his Kingdom; and that he permitted the darnel (another's seed) to remain near his Kingdom: that was the mystery within the comparison's design.

A paradoxical situation: God sowed wheat. And he permitted a maneuver: forces dangerous to his crop entered into play. This is the beginning of a conflict—which is central to the parable—represented by the Master's attitude and that of his servants.

The servants are intrigued. They appear to suspect the farmer of negligence. "Have you sorted the seed well?"[1] Then, when they knew that he was the victim of his enemy, they were full of zeal, but out of season. Opposite this, the parable places the clear-sightedness of the Master: "Some enemy has done this . . . ," and his patience: "Let them both grow till the harvest; and at harvest time I shall say to the reapers . . . ."

Evil, since the beginning of time, has taken up

residence in the work of God; the same situation must endure until the consummation. Such is the Master of the Harvest's design.

By means of the parable we must shape ourselves according to God's ideology, see with his eyes, submit our intelligence to his.

We will have to harmonize two attitudes, which at first glance, would appear contradictory: an absolute intransigence toward a work which is not that of God; an unshakable patience in order to preserve our optimism.

Intransigence. It is well to know our place. To choose our place. To be wheat, in a bold and resolute manner. For one day the curtain will fall at the conclusion of the play: "As it was in Noah's day, so will it also be in the days of the Son of Man. People were eating and drinking, marrying wives and husbands, right up to the day Noah went into the ark, and the Flood came and destroyed them all. It will be the same as it was in Lot's day: people were eating and drinking, buying and selling, planting and building, but the day Lot left Sodom, God rained fire and brimstone from heaven and it destroyed them all. It will be the same when the day comes for the Son of Man to be revealed. When that day comes, anyone on the housetop, with his possessions in the house, must not come down to collect them, nor must anyone in the fields turn back either" (Luke 17:26-31).

Thus let us have no weakness, no connivance for

evil. "If we wish to serve (both) God and the world, it will be to our detriment. What does it profit a man if he gains the world and loses his soul? The present world and the next world, which is ours, are two enemies. The present world advocates adultery, corruption, avarice, fraud—and the next world renounces these crimes. Thus we cannot be friends with both. We must renounce the first and live for the other. We believe that it is better to hate the things of this world, because they are of little importance, of short duration, corruptible, and to love the other things, the incorruptible values" (Clement of Rome).

Thus spoke the ancients at a time when the Roman empire was the embodiment of the Beast (as presented in the book of Revelation). Such an era excuses one for identifying the "world" with Evil. It is a unilateral view of things; another prejudice would be to exorcize totally the modern world.

Possessing a Christianity more firmly established than that of the third Pope of Rome does not exempt us from being clear-sighted. In his time, one could not conceive that Caesar might become a Christian. Today we are astonished at the enmity of many governments. Throughout the entire history of the Church, political totalitarianism has never disarmed. To preserve her Christian savor for the masses, there were in every age Christians living in the deserts, or in monastic cells or in convents, or else making a cell out of their solitude of mind and heart. Because the Kingdom is not the world; and as there are men given over to the world, there must be men belonging to the Kingdom—to nothing but the Kingdom.

And **patience.** The separation, of which we are speaking, is above all one of principles. Paul, in his day, found himself faced with the necessity of compromise. In order to shun idolatry, to escape contact with the licentious, it is necessary to leave this world, he wrote to the Corinthians. Christians cannot do this. What is more, we are at a period when the human eye distinguishes with difficulty the wheat from the darnel. Sometimes one smells the demoniacal. As a general rule, innumerable "buts" and "ifs" conceal from us the profound reality, that of God. The wheat presents its blemishes and its illnesses; worldly principles slip into it. The darnel has undeniably human qualities, and intentions can be good when results are disastrous.

The present situation, such as it is, enters into God's plan. He wills it in the interest of everyone. In our interest, for he is sure that if we remain firm in the faith, the presence of the "bad" at our side will engender patience, and this is already hope. We aspire to the time of the harvest. Moreover, does not the proximity of the darnel help the wheat to rise up more firm and more sturdy? One leaves trees in closed-in nurseries; an oak grows well only in the forest.

Above all, let us not meddle by trying to do the discriminatory work of the last days. Judgment, in the final analysis, belongs only to God. God is

jealous of his right to judge. Our human hands are
too clumsy; our eyes see badly, hindered by the
superficiality of things.

A place, therefore, for patience. St. Jerome, the
great dualist, who returned with good measure the
blows dealt to him, is obliged to yield place to
patience; and we are warned, he explains, not to
precipitate the fall of a brother; for it can happen
that he who is today corrupted by a dangerous doctrine may come tomorrow to repentance and begin
to defend the truth. A beautiful canvas upon which
St. Peter Chrysologus embellishes: "Today's darnel
can change tomorrow into wheat; thus the heretic of
today will be one of the faithful tomorrow; he who
until the present has shown himself a sinner, henceforth will be joined to the just. If the patience of
God came not to the aid of the darnel, the Church
would possess neither the evangelist Matthew—it was
necessary to take him from among the tax collectors—
nor the apostle Paul; it was necessary to take him
from among the persecutors. Is it not true that
Ananias (from the book of Acts) sought to uproot the
wheat, when, sent by God to Saul, he accused St.
Paul in this manner: Lord, how much harm he has
done to your saints! (That means to say: uproot the
darnel.) Why send me, the sheep, to the wolf? Me,
the pious man, to the accursed? Why send a missionary of size to the persecutor? While Ananias
spoke of the persecutor, the Lord knew that here
was a missionary. And at the moment that Ananias
judged him as the darnel of hell, he was for Christ

a chosen vessel, and he was already placed within the heavenly granery." (Sermon 97.)

Real time is that of God's patience and of our repentance.

I wonder if we are not unfaithful to Our Lord's thinking by stopping such a long time on the subject of the darnel. It is in the wheat's interest that God refuses to uproot the darnel: Be afraid, while gathering the darnel, that you might uproot the wheat with it. The time which is given at the same time to the wheat and to the darnel is the time of growth; whether God prolongs it or shortens it, it is always for his elect (Mark 13:20). It is neither cruelty nor egoism to speak thus. While concentrating on the divine intention, which passionately desires saints, and submitting thoroughly to it, we pity the darnel, and we collaborate in its transformation. If all Catholics had always been enlightened saints, would there be so many unfaithful?

That which God notices and loves is the wheat; this is to say, his Word, which sprouted in human hearts and there became contemplation, love, holiness, sacrifice; his Word, which must still grow, incarnate in the holiness of Christian families, as in the martyrdom of so many of our brothers today; his Word, which will make the enthusiasm of contemporary youth ripen.

There you have what God loves and notices, above what fills the newspapers or what the airwaves spread from one end of the world to another. He does not fear competition from artificial satellites. His stars are not frightened by electric light. No more so does he scorn it, for it is his creation.

Let us keep clear heads during the fleeting whirlwinds that provoke the earth. Each time that the Church has been tempted by the intoxication of a purely human advancement, she has corrected herself—she will always correct herself—in order to repeat Our Lord's reply to temptation: Man does not live by bread alone, but by each word that comes from the mouth of God.

Gazing upon his wheatfield, God feels love and pride, like the farmer who in days gone by went out after Sunday Vespers to tour and admire his crops. The Creator, confronting the beauty of the material world which had just gone forth from his hands, ". . . saw that the light was good"; and when he had made all plants and fruit trees sprout, "he saw that it was good." Do you not believe that he repeats these words after each of his spiritual creations, at each new thrust of life and light in his field, the Church? He is proud of his saints.

One day Satan presented himself in the council which God holds with his angels: "Where have you been?"

"Round the earth."

"Did you notice my servant Job? There is no one like him on the earth: a sound and honest man who fears God and shuns evil."

The Seed Growing by Itself (Mark 4:26-29)

"This is what the kingdom of God is like. A man throws seed on the land. Night and day, while he sleeps, when he is awake, the seed is sprouting and growing; how, he does not know. Of its own accord the land produces first the shoot, then the ear, then the full grain in the ear. And when the crop is ready, he loses no time: he starts to reap because the harvest has come."

Two scenes mingle before Our Lord's eyes. On the first level—the countrysides each year are covered with crops; on the second level—the harvest of souls: "Look around you, look at the fields; already they are white, ready for harvest!" (John 4:35). The spiritual harvest grows along with the temporal harvest. The same source of light and heat—for God is the sun of souls and the visible sun symbolizes him—makes the two crops ripen.

Some mystics also have received the gift of double sight. A St. Francis of Assisi, a St. Hildegard of Bingen contemplate directly, in nature, the activity of God. The world is his raiment. His footprints are everywhere visible, and the mystical lover tracks him down. "The footprints imprinted in things permitted St. Francis to follow the Beloved everywhere; in order to climb to the throne of God, he made a ladder out of all creatures" (Thomas of Celano).

Confronted in our time by our progress in the understanding of the cosmos, of the secrets of matter, of life, of human existence, and beyond this with our techniques and methods of scientific investigation (to which is bound an unheard of blossoming of learning), enthusiasm takes hold of us. Such an enthusiasm, as the ancients recognized in their day, bears an essentially religious character. It depends upon our freedom and upon God's gift whether it develops into a genuine Christian mystique, the preparation for our eschatological fulfillment.

From now on, in any case, all Christians have the capacity for ultimate sanctification as a result of their efforts. Whether it be in science or in a more material order, all work collaborates with creation; nothing deviates from the direction of God's Kingdom.

The secret of faith will be to find God, or to introduce him at every moment into the elements and events of the world which, to all appearances, have nothing to do with his supernatural design.

The farmer cast his seed on the land. He is finished; his task is accomplished. He no longer thinks about his land, but attends to his daily needs. The wheat sprouts without his intervention, without his attention, without his realizing it. The earth bears fruit by itself. The lesson is hiding in the farmer's freedom from care. The Kingdom grows like the temporal harvest. Never is the farmer's hope frustrated. Thus, desire for the Kingdom will lead humanity to the harvest. Jesus reveals to us the certitude which fills his soul and which assures him of the success of his message. We must not hurry the decisive hour. As surely as it will come, as unrestrainedly, unavoidably, God prepares it in the

secrecy of his activity. Jesus could have repeated his
parable to his disciples James and John when they
proposed to call down fire from heaven upon the
inhospitable Samaritans (Luke 9:52-55). Demonstra-
tions of force are not conducive to the establishment
of God's Kingdom.

In the face of laws of inertia which appear to
hamper God's work, arises, in all its majesty, the law
of an irresistible power that uplifts creation toward
its Creator.

Once we are firmly anchored in a good mental
attitude, certain of the necessary advancement of
the Kingdom in the world, within us and through
us—all this is the same—we will at the same time
find optimism again and freedom from care.

Optimism blends with joy and peace: the fruits of
the Holy Spirit. ". . . through our Lord Jesus Christ,
by faith we are judged righteous and at peace with
God."[2] This is Jesus' optimism. The victory of his
word was assured, in spite of the apparent obscurity
which enveloped it: one does not bring in a lamp to
put it under a bushel.

"For there is nothing hidden but it must be disclosed, nothing kept secret except to be brought to
light" (Mark 4:21-22).

"What I say to you in the dark, tell in the day-
light; what you hear in whispers, proclaim from the
housetops" (Matt. 10:27).

The victory of prayer is just as certain: "Ask and
you shall receive." The strength of his Church and

her victory over antagonistic forces are assured. Faith will always be victorious. Jesus' optimism grew into joy: "There is one thing in Christ's life that he hides. I have often thought that it was his joy" (Chesterton).

St. Paul and all the great saints, the great believers, share this optimism. St. Paul is the great leader of faith. Defeatism does not measure up to his theology of salvation: he who has chosen us is himself power and fidelity. If he has chosen us, he will carry out his gift to completion; he will glorify us. "Christian" and "Saint" are equivalent titles. Thus holiness for St. Paul is not an extraordinary phenomenon. What is abnormal is that there could be anything else but saints. What is abnormal is a fearful, anemic Christianity waiting for one knows not what kind of blood transfusion from a new civilization, when we are the salt of the earth, the light of the world. Holiness is the journey begun at baptism that should draw to an end, one day, in heaven. At baptism we took certain pledges; we renew them at least once. Are we bearing in mind that God himself, on that day, took a solemn pledge to save us? And to save many others along with us? This is why cries of optimism scan the letters of the apostle Paul. Unquestionably he explained to us in Romans the tragic part of human existence: we will never be the saints of which we dreamed. However, he concludes on a triumphant note: "With God on our side who can be against us? Since God did not spare his own Son . . . we may be certain . . . that he will not refuse anything he can give. Could anyone accuse those whom God has

chosen?" (Who will separate us from the love of
Christ which surrounds us like the combined love of
a father and mother?) "For I am certain of this:
neither death nor life, no angel, no prince, nothing
that exists, nothing still to come, . . . nor any created
thing, can ever come between us and the love of God
made visible in Christ Jesus our Lord" (Rom. 8:31-39).

Optimism and confidence extend to temporal life.
God makes flowers bloom and the grass of the fields
sprout; he feeds the birds. How could he be disinterested in our carnal lives? "Think of the flowers
growing in the fields; they never have to work or
spin; yet I assure you that not even Solomon in all
his regalia was robed like one of these" (Matt. 6:28-29).

Freedom from care normally accompanies confidence in God. After all, to assure the success of the
Church, of our sanctity, of our labors whatever they
may be, is not our business but God's. Very simply,
it is enough for us to accomplish our task as Christians. The man in the parable let the crop sprout by
itself: he is a man without cares, comments Maldonat.
Such is the freedom from care of the great Condé,
who has prepared everything for the next day's battle
and who sleeps; such, the heedlessness of St. Peter
Canisius, who would continue to play billiards if
someone announced his approaching death to him.
This is a lack of care which puts human activity in its
true place. The Christian task is perfectly in harmony
with this freedom from care: the task of the good
workers who "each year work the same land with
the same care, in the sight of God, and plant them."

Or else even the games of little girls: "The innocence of children is the greatest glory of God. Everything one does during the day is pleasing to God, provided naturally that it is as it should be" (Péguy).

According to the parable we are witnessing a growth in maturity. The entire world, all generations, space and time are encompassed by this wheatfield which grows and ripens in a few months, once and for all. We ourselves seek the phenomenon of a linear extension in time, generations which succeed each other, harvests that are renewed year after year. We seek the advancement and the enlargement of the Kingdom, pressured by time. Surely God is correct. True progress is found in the nontemporal, particularly in the increase of saints and in the maturation of the spiritual life in the totality of Christians of all eras.

"The Church serenely lengthens the list of her saints," wrote Father Rousselot. "Different and all admirable, magnanimous and humble of heart, austere and sweet, they pass through the midst of men who often persecute them and almost always disdain them. But how they cry out to souls as, martyrs and mystics, they remain on earth the witnesses of God, the continuators of Christ, the heroes of the Spirit."

Basically, they are always the same saints. It is as if one generation alone produced them, all dissimilar like the leaves of a great tree, like the stalks in the wheatfield, yet basically all so similar, because all reproduce Christ. They have been seen by God in this similitude. "They are the ones he chose specially long ago and intended to become true images of his Son, so that his Son might be the eldest of many brothers" (Rom. 8:29).[3]

Charity will always be the same, a pulsation of God's great love. All ways of being a saint are the same. A single rhythm directs the efforts of the best among Christians for attaining God through love. After the founders of sanctity—those inimitable and compelling models: Jesus, in a unique position, then Paul, John, and the apostles—these are the epigoni: martyr saints like St. Ignatius of Antioch (". . . myself, though I am the prisoner of Christ and though I may contemplate the things of heaven and the hierarchies of angels, the phalanxes of principalities, things visible and invisible, I am not yet for that reason a true disciple"—he had not yet been gnawed by the wild animals of the amphitheater); those of the intellectual and theological mysticism of the Alexandrian School: (Let one purify one's intelligence through asceticism and then, throwing aside the "last veil," see the divine splendor shining brightly as in a mirror; only then is one truly man, and by the same action, the perfect image of God, the temple of the Holy Trinity, the Word of God by grace.); all the monks with their abnegation of self-will summed up in obedience to superiors; and then the saints of the "apostolic life"; those of the "evangelical life" who encourage the return to remote sources; the saints of more recent mystical tradition; the pilgrim saints; the hermit saints; then the host who belong to no school . . . .

Our growth is necessary to God. Normally the

germ of sanctity deposited in our soul will grow to consummate sanctity, but our collaboration with grace is always implied. This is why, without doubt, our parable inspired the first attempts at a systematization of the stages in a "spiritual" life. Let us listen to St. Gregory the Great: "Man throws seed upon the land when he plants a good intention [a good desire] in his heart. And that done, he should, taking rest in hope, rely upon God. He lies down at night and arises in the morning, for he makes headway in the midst of successes and failures. The seed sprouts and grows without his knowing, because, though he cannot yet reap the fruit of its progress, virtue once set in motion marches toward its fulfillment. The earth bears fruit on its own because the soul of man, predisposed by grace, rises toward the fruit of good works. But this same land produces first the shoot, then the ear, then the full grain in the ear. To produce the sprout is to still feel how weak good will is. At the stage of the ears, this is virtue which grows and impels us to increase our good works. The full grain is when virtue has made such progress that one has arrived at the fullness of action and of constancy in the accomplishment of duty. When the fruit is ripe, one wields the scythe, because all is God's crop, his harvest which belongs to him."

[1]Jerusalem Bible: "Was it not good seed that you sowed . . .?" (Matt. 13:27).

[2]French text, literally: "Have peace with God through Our Lord Jesus Christ."

[3]The French text adds the phrase: "of which he was given as the pattern." (Trans. note: This phrase does not appear in the Vulgate.)

II

THE ANTITHESIS
OF THE KINGDOM

The planting period and that of harvesting are not only distinct, but they oppose each other according to a fundamental antithesis, which is according to the divine plan. As greatly as the harvest will reveal all the glory of God's Kingdom, that much does the planting underscore its earthly precariousness. In order that the final glory of the Kingdom may be entirely God's, is it not proper that what is destined to become so great begins on earth in "mystery" and "littleness"?

The Mustard Seed

(Matt. 13:31-32; cf. Mark 4:30-32 and Luke 13:18-19)

"The kingdom of heaven is like a mustard seed which a man took and sowed in his field. It is the smallest of all the seeds, but when it has grown it is the biggest shrub of all and becomes a tree so that the birds of the air come and shelter in its branches."

Botanists tell us that the plant referred to is the black mustard. "The plant is well known in Palestine, where in hot areas, as for example near the Sea of Galilee or along the Jordan, it reaches the dimensions of a tree ten to thirteen feet high and even becomes woody at its base. This is the black mustard (**Brassica nigra**) of our botanists. Goldfinches, especially, who appear very partial to black mustard seeds, come in flocks to perch on the branches of this tree (the Arabs say: mustard tree) and eat the seeds" (Biever).

But knowledgeable explanations risk veiling the deep meaning. For example, independent of ornithologists, we know the birds of our parable. They are those of Nebuchadnezzar's dream: "I saw a tree in the middle of the world; it was very tall. The tree grew taller and stronger, until its top reached the sky, and it could be seen from the ends of the earth. . . . the birds of heaven nested in its branches" (Dan. 4:7-9).

The tree is born in the Garden of Eden; it accompanies the history of the great Eastern empires, all more or less messianic. It will be the Kingdom of the Messiah, and it depicts the Messiah himself. We find it again in Ezekiel (31:3-6), in the book of Daniel, and it has just reappeared in the Dead Sea Psalms: "Its shadow will overshadow the entire world, its top will reach to heaven and its roots down to hell" (Hymn VI:15-16). It is also, God knows by what poetic alchemy, the oak of LaFontaine: "Whose head was the neighbor of heaven and whose feet touched down in the kingdom of the dead."

The meaning of the parable is all in the antithesis between the smallness of the seed and the height of the tree. It reveals the law of synthesis that rules the

Kingdom: the mediocrity of its beginnings promises the flowering of the eschatological Kingdom. More than once Our Lord had to encourage his disciples, alarmed by the failure of their work and by the threats that weighed upon it: "There is no need to be afraid, little flock, for it has pleased your Father to give you the kingdom" (Luke 12:32). It is on one of these occasions that he tells them the parable. They were in the hands of God: mediocre beginning, seed, branch cut from the tree of Judaism. The entire strength of the future was within these beginnings. In the divine logic, their weakness conditioned the future greatness of the Kingdom they carried within themselves. Every religious soul understands this reverse logic.

From the initial weakness to the final grandeur there is not, according to the manner of thinking which we must assimilate, a true biological development. Two realities follow upon each other: the seed and the great tree are in opposition to each other much more than they are naturally coordinated. In the same way as we see the small seed now, one day we will see the tree.

The choice itself of a small seed carries with it the choice of the type of plant. Jesus could have taken a fig tree, or a vine, or a palm tree—a veritable tree, as the traditional method did—if he had not wanted precisely to underscore the weakness of the Kingdom's beginnings. It is that which gave scandal and which constitutes the initial secret of the divine plan.

We must harden ourselves, within our modern perspective, in order to place the second accent of the parable upon eschatological grandeur (with which the antithesis will truly be made), in the times in which we live: a weakness, a state of mediocrity—the payment for future glory. Since the Discourse on Universal History, one too often identifies the great tree with the Church of today. "For us," wrote a great exegete, "the precept has the appearance of a prophecy realized. History makes us present at the humble beginnings and at the development of God's reign, from era to era, passing from hostile Jews to contemptuous pagans. We have only to open our eyes to see it established in the entire world, according a shelter to so many souls who live for God, inviting and waiting for the peoples who will want to obtain his justice and savor his word" (Lagrange).

It would be unfair to insist. Father Lagrange understood very well when he left historical exegesis to approach the shores of apologetics. And he knew, as well if not better than we, that this Kingdom of God which he described recalled a little too much the nationalistic and earthly messianism of latter-day Judaism. It was from this perspective only that Jewish exegesis allegorized: the birds represented the pagans; they were seen taking refuge with their riches in a renovated Jerusalem, infinitely enlarged and glorified. For Jesus, the messianic kingdom was only the earthly debut of the "Kingdom of heaven." It is inseparable from its eternal completion; it is already spiritual. The birds of the air are in accord with its celestial dignity. The greatness of the Church is in its heavenly essence. It is not realized in magnificence of the human order.

But to what degree does glory truly belong to the Church of today? Is she closer to her goal than to the lowliness of the planting? We are touching upon the mystery of God. But when one thinks about what will one day be the completion, when the form of this world will "pass away," all possible worldly "magnificence" vanishes. How could Our Lord, who "knows," who comes forth from the divine majesty, offer a "grandeur" in this world for our admiration? Were it more splendid than all we imagine, it would remain ephemeral, unstable, at an infinite distance from the heavenly future. There is the great tree! Considering the passage of time in relation to eternity, everything temporal remains at the point of departure. We are always departing as long as we have not arrived.

Littleness, grandeur in secret: this was the understanding of the Fathers. They always define the earthly state of God's Kingdom by a principle of humility here below. Sometimes it is Christ himself: ". . . the Lord compared himself to a mustard seed, the most bitter and smallest of seeds, but whose power and influence is stimulated by sufferings and persecutions . . ." (Hilary); sometimes it is the faith, sometimes the martyrs (Ambrose), sometimes the humble preaching of the gospel (Jerome). St. Paul sounded the note:

"Take yourselves for instance, brothers, at the time when you were called: how many of you were wise in the ordinary sense of the word, how many were influential people, or came from noble families? No, it was to shame the wise that God chose what is foolish by human reckoning, and to shame what is strong that he chose what is weak by human reckoning; those whom the world thinks common and contemptible are the ones that God has chosen—those who are nothing at all to show up those who are everything" (1 Cor. 1:26-28).

The Church will remain great within her weakness. If it were necessary to choose between Christianity under Nero and Diocletian, and the times of Constantine; between the blood of St. Agnes and the purple of a Theodora, what Christian would hesitate? The day when the Church made the conquest of the Roman empire, she was overcome by it. St. Augustine lived during that dramatic period when Christians were converted **en masse:** "After the persecutions, so numerous and so cruel, when, peace having come, the pagan crowds (desirous of taking the name of Christian) found an obstacle to the custom they had of celebrating the feasts of their false gods with sumptuous meals and drunkenness, and could not easily deprive themselves of these pernicious and deep-rooted pleasures, our predecessors, to sacrifice something, thought well to replace pagan feasts with other feasts in honor of martyr saints, which one could celebrate without sacrilege, although with the same excesses. But now is the time when those who no longer dare refuse to be Christians set about living according to the will of Christ. If they are Christians, may they set aside the concessions which have been made for them in order to become so."

At similar moments the anchorites, the monks, begin to live according to the Gospel again. St. Benedict, in the grotto at Subiaco, is the mustard seed. The monastic rules, recapturing the ideal of life in Gospel times, returned to the nucleus of the Twelve—to the little band, to the first community in Jerusalem with its poverty, its charity. Later, the mendicant orders relighted the torch: "Obey the Holy Gospel." In humility, sow within self the mustard seed.

St. Jerome described in an unforgettable Latin the weakness of our doctrine: "**Praedicatio evangelii minima est omnibus disciplinis.** The preaching of the gospel is the most lowly among intellectual theories. This doctrine, from the very first, appears absurd, when it preaches a man who would be God, and a dead God, and the scandal of the cross. Compare this doctrine to the teachings of philosophers and their books, to the bursting forth of their eloquence and to the perfect order of their discourse, and you will see to what degree the gospel seed is smaller than other seeds."

Let us replace philosophy by modern sociology, and eloquence by the propaganda that wins over the world, and we will be able to see that the Gospel doctrine has remained a tiny thing. But this weakness is that of a teaching stripped of the accessory of human finery and made to deliver a human heart to God. For that it is necessary to erect a cross.

Our recruiting is worthy of our doctrine. "The first visitors of the incarnate Word were the shepherds and the Magi," remarks Mgr. Benson. "The shepherds of Bethlehem and the wise men of the East can kneel before his cradle: the simplest and the wisest. The simplest, that is to say those who are accustomed to silence, to the stars, to birth and death; those who possess none of the notions that can so easily obscure clear-sightedness. The wisest, that is to say those who had arrived at the limits of the wisdom of that time (though, concerning the physical world having, without doubt, infinitely less knowledge than the smallest of present-day schoolboys), who were as cultivated and educated as it was possible to be at their epoch, who could encompass at a glance the worlds of knowledge they had explored, and understand to what poverty of results they had attained. The individuals of these last two classes were in no wise tempted to believe that they knew what this was. The science they had acquired led them only to conclude that they were ignorant of everything."

But there will always be more of the poor than of the wise in the Church; and the wise enter it only through the door of weakness. "The more I plunge into the mystery of nature," said Pasteur, "the more my faith becomes simple. Already it resembles the faith of a Breton peasant; I have a thousand reasons for believing that, if I can descend still more deeply, it will become like that of the peasant's wife."

We do not yet like to look upon the weakness of our Church in the midst of this world's powers. Indeed, she has made numerous friends here; but her enemies are formidable. Why still preserve the illusion that persecutions have ceased since the conversion of the Roman emperors to Christianity? History has need of a certain recoil, less perhaps in order to commend those who have given all for their faith—whether members of the clergy or the most lowly of the faithful—than to keep from condemning those who were not up to the standard of heroic times.

Could the Church be sufficiently humble if we did not form it out of the humility of all of our personal humilities?

Thus let us receive the small seed of the Kingdom in a soul which is proportionately small. The vitality of our spiritual life hinges upon an admitted weakness: "It is when I am weak that I am strong." Let us not fear, in spite of all the noise of this world, to wrap ourselves in the silence of the inner life. Prayer, conversation with God, renunciation of human grandiloquence for the joys of contemplation: there is the Christian's call. Let us give first place in our anxieties to these old, unfashionable things. To speak and be active for the Kingdom is good; to pray is better. Speeches and works will be made good only through prayer: "You also, explains Theophylactus, "may be the mustard seed which seems so

small. It is not a question of praising oneself for
virtuous acts, but of showing oneself fervent, inciting
others by that fervor, censuring them by our austerity.
. . . One must be perfect among the weak and the
imperfect."

Should it be necessary to remind Christians that
suffering always remains on the horizon of all earthly
existence? Christ's disciple suffers like the others, but
accepts difficulty with joy, according to the measure
of his holiness. He accepts sorrows and vexations as
things due him, which put him in his true place:
"This is why I delight in my weaknesses, my humilia-
tions, my miseries, my persecutions, my tribulations:
for Christ."

To know that the Kingdom of God rises on the
horizon, in proportion as weakness is displayed, is to
accept being the mustard seed. . . . Our grandfathers
themselves manufactured their mustard. In a corner
of the garden, black mustard plants grew and re-
seeded themselves each year. They gathered the
seeds and crushed them in a large bowl by rolling
them with a cannon ball picked up on some battle-
field. Let us have the courage to imitate them in
spiritual things, and through faith and the courage
to toil and suffer, reanimate the natural virtue of the
mustard seed (cf. Hilaire).

Parable of the Yeast (Matt. 13:33; cf. Luke 13:20-21)

Matthew closely unites the parable of the yeast
with that of the mustard seed. We will therefore
have to interpret it likewise by the contrast between

the trifle which the yeast is, in the light of the bread we will obtain.

"The kingdom of heaven is like the yeast a woman took and mixed in with three measures of flour till it was leavened all through."

The leaven of which we are speaking is not an "assimilatory" force. It is only a common piece of raised and sour dough that one will put into the flour. Our Lord is interested, not in the internal behavior of the phenomenon of fermentation, but in the visible change: at the outset this bit of raised dough, and at the end, the entire mass—the extraordinary mass comprised of three leavened measures, so much more than the normal batch: it would suffice at a dinner for one hundred persons. Jeremias justly underscores its relationship with the parable of the mustard seed, where the mustard becomes a great tree, with the same end, which is to show that it is a question of divine realities.

A suggestive word: the woman **hides** the leaven in the flour.[1] This piece of dough is so small that it passes unperceived, and this suffices. This is our contrast between the smallness of the beginnings of the Kingdom and the final grandeur, the final grandeur being promised by the beginnings. The "little flock" will become the Kingdom (Luke 12:32). This beginning, like the little flock from the desert, no one will notice. But its smallness already hides its future glory, contains it germinally.

"Hidden" is contrasted with "leavened all through";

that is to say concretely, all the raised dough, visibly "raised," in the parable. "For there is nothing hidden [by God] but it must be disclosed . . .'" (Mark 4:22). "No one lights a lamp and puts it in some hidden place or under a tub, but on the lamp-stand . . ." (Luke 11:33).

It is always, very definitely, the same beginning for the Kingdom: a little flock, a mustard seed, a bit of leaven, a small lighted lamp—even new wine; one does not put new wine in old skins. It is always God's work, so lowly in its beginnings. And always, in conformity with its beginnings, God, who "sees in secret," and for this "secret" itself, promises to that work the future glory of his Kingdom, which will gush out (but always in secret) upon all the advances in the Church's work. The advances will be visible in a human establishment, the messianic Kingdom; but this establishment has true value only in as much as it carries the secret of its future greatness.

The Gospel of Thomas, recently discovered in the Coptic manuscripts of Nag-Hammadi and momentarily advanced to an exaggerated celebrity, understood well the general idea of the parable. It set the parable forth in its own way: "The Kingdom of the Father is like unto a woman: she took a bit of leaven, hid it in some dough, and made of it large loaves of bread." A little piece of leaven at the start, large loaves of bread at the finish. This is the classical antithesis of parables of the Kingdom. Moreover, the large loaves of bread in that Gospel are the unprecedented developments promised in the **secret** science

of the Gnostics. The introductory formula, "the Kingdom of the Father" warned us that we were entering
the esoteric domain of Gnosticism.

An exegesis current today puts the accent on the
virtue which the leaven releases: "The parable of the
mustard seed revealed to us the future expansion of
the kingdom; that of the leaven tells us of its
mysterious virtue" (Valensin-Huby). "It will be for
Christianity in the world as for the leaven in the
dough: a divine force, hidden and silent, but active,
contagious, coming gradually nearer and nearer, and
assimilatory, until the point where, under its action,
all humanity may be raised up for the service and
glory of God. On that day, in the same way that the
dough became savoury through its fermentation, the
entire world, transformed by the gospel, will have re-
gained the complacency of its creator, because it will
itself have again found a taste for the things of God"
(Durand).

[1]The French text, literally: ". . . which a woman has taken
and hidden in three measures of flour. . . ."

III

THE ENCOUNTER
WITH THE KINGDOM

The man who encounters the Kingdom on his journey is wholly transformed. "The time has come," Jesus said, "and the kingdom of God is close at hand. Repent, and believe the Good News" (Mark 1:15). He who believes in the Good News must know that he has found a treasure. In other Gospel terms, he has entered into the Kingdom; he permits the Kingdom to enter into him and conquer him, body and soul. Nothing counts more from now on: temporal goods, the search for human justice, confidence in self, in his own merits—he renounces all these for the superior good which replaces them.

The Treasure and the Pearl (Matt. 13:44-45)

"The kingdom of heaven is like treasure hidden in a field which someone has found; he hides it again, goes off happy, sells everything he owns and buys the field.

"Again, the kingdom of heaven is like a merchant looking for fine pearls; when he finds one of great value he goes and sells everything he owns and buys it."

Nothing is comparable to this treasure or to that

fine pearl. Joy transports the man who had made the find. No longer does anything count until he has acquired the treasure field or the incomparable stone.

Can we notice a difference between the two brief stories? The Talmud tells us of fortuitous discoveries of treasures: "Abba Judan betook himself to Antioch to work the second part of his field. While he worked, the soil opened in front of him, and his cow fell into the hole, breaking a leg during her fall. He went down into the hole to pull his beast out. At that moment God opened his eyes and he found a treasure there. He said: It is for my good that my cow broke her leg." One finds a treasure as if by accident. Did not one search for it? There are archeologists with trained eyes. "Always it is that in Palestine, more than elsewhere, the popular imagination is haunted by the thought of treasures to discover. How many times has the farmer who works his field, or spades his garden, clandestinely carried out greedy searches, his heart hoping for **amphorae** filled with antiquities" (Buzy). It is thought that one of the volumes preserved at Qumran was a sort of guide for treasure hunters.

In any case, the merchant is in quest of precious pearls. His business is to search. The windfall always remains a chance, but one must be a professional to recognize it in an oriental bazaar.

Every grace of the Kingdom shares in two formulas. It is always unexpected, even when one looks for it; one cannot imagine what it will be before having

received it. It is always looked for, even when one
is not aware of searching, for there is a profound
good will: **irrequietum est cor nostrum.**

The whole thing is "to find." We are not truly
Christians until the day we have discovered that the
Kingdom is "everything" in our life, more indis-
pensable than our daily bread: the water from a
gushing fountain that quenches the thirst once and
for all. Every deep religious life passes through one
or more experiences which resemble "conversions."
This is the word of the Gospel, the bearer of joy:
"The time has come and the kingdom of God is close
at hand. Be converted, and believe the Good News."

What one calls conversions are perhaps not such
in the proper sense of the word, except for the dramatic element which they include. They help us to
discover ourselves being acted upon by grace.

Charles de Foucauld merits consideration for the
profoundly human quality of his experience, his
disquietude, his period of trouble, his need for solitude, for researching the great problems of God and
the hereafter; "he searched for the light and did not
find it." His biographer continues: "But in Charles'
soul, the tide of grace rose. At first one does not
know where it comes from. It is promised to men
of good will, or rather, it is already given to them,
and their good will itself is its work. At the moment
when it seems distant, it has already covered the
slimy sea-bed; it is fresh; it brings its birds with it,
and its waves that unfurl one after another, all of

them saying: one must believe! Be joyful because of the great divine joy, and receive the light upon living waters. He felt that obscure movement, that desire for illumination within himself, becoming more and more powerful" (René Bazin).

At the beginning of this century autobiographies of converts multiplied: Protestants, men of action, scholars. Albert von Ruville sought the highest form of liberty in the Catholic Church; one can come as near to God as one wishes: one can act, serve God, do penance, offer sacrifices in one's own way. This is the unlimited liberty (for becoming holy). Robert Hugh Benson finds absolute peace of mind in Catholicism. Nearer to us, some Protestants have come to the Church attracted by its liturgy or its sacraments. Still today, one relives the adventure of St. Justin: "I have successively studied all the sciences. I have concluded by stopping at the doctrine of the Christians, although it displeases those who are won over by error." To these converts one could apply St. Hilary's remark: "A long and painful labor is required to attain to the knowledge of the pearl."

Ernest Psichari, having refused all moral discipline, imposes military discipline upon himself, after the manner of a desert mystic, in Mauritania. "Men accustomed to the noonday sun, men with direct eyes, with glad hearts, you who know the desert and the oasis in the desert, who know a country where there is no one, and where there is nothing. . . . Latin, Roman, French, heir to the Roman way, camp builder, you who know what it is to blaze a trail and to pitch a camp. To build a road and to build a camp. You who know what the desert is and what travel on camel-back is. You who alone among us have heard silence. In the solitude of three or four months. And who thus have maintained purity of soul. . . ." He publishes his confessions: **The Voices Who Cry in the Wilderness,** then **Journey of the Centurion.** " 'Finally,' says Maxentius [the centurion] 'nothing can do it. Twenty centuries separate him from the Moors. That power, whose mark he bears, is what recaptured the sands for the crescent of Islam, and it is what drags along the immense cross upon his shoulders. . . .' " The treasure sometimes seems to him like a mirage in the desert. His guide, Sidia, says to him one day: " 'I know that Issa [Jesus] is a great prophet, but what do you say, you other Nazarene, about him?' I did not hesitate a minute," writes Psichari, "and I answered Sidia: 'Issa, my friend, is not a prophet, but in all truth, he is the Son of God. . . .' " But at this point he stops, his throat tight, his eyes filled with tears. "Was this wonderful story mine? Had I the right to make it mine, to confess Jesus Christ, without believing?" He falls on his knees, understanding that one does not struggle against this mysterious force, and says "softly, like a very tired hiker at the end of the day: 'My God, I am speaking to you; listen to me. Have pity on me; no one has taught me how to pray to you. But I say to you, as your Son told us to say to you—I say to you with all my heart as my fathers have said to you in times past: Our Father who art in heaven.' "

The decisive moment for a soul can take the direction of total disbelief. From the depths of discouragement or despair, faith seems like the treasure one does not look for—gratuitous, so gratuitous that it was impossible even to look for it: if not, it would not have been gratuitous. Faith seems to be the sole reason for living. Or rather: it **is** the sole reason for living. For example, Mounier. An attack of doubt of the classic type in his youth: a religion halted at a childish stage becomes insufficient. Meanwhile the rest of the man pursues its course. Completely downcast, then rendered immune for life by "an intellectual and religious reconversion . . . starting from scratch." In order to live, he accepts himself as he is: "Basically, a man of faith, even in constitution and temperament. . . . One of those men who are made for believing. . . . All that is theirs is good for a further building of the edifice, for adding to the interior light—not for placing in question, at each moment, the total picture. . . . This interior strength, palpable as it was, gave me a continuity, an interior fidelity in my conversation with the world, which preserved me from continual confusion and despair."

In his joy, the man who found the treasure went out to sell **all** he possessed.

The saints comprise the category of those who have the heroic courage and the joy to sell everything at once. Peter: "Lord, we have left everything to follow you." Paul: "Since the time that it pleased God to reveal his Son in me, I have not noticed either flesh or blood." Francis of Assisi sold Foligno the bolts of material and his father's horse, explaining: "I have left the century." Psichari wished to "recover the chalice that had slipped from infidel hands." But the year was 1914. The 22nd of August, Lieutenant Psichari gave his blood for France at Rossignol, his rosary wrapped around his wrist.

Taking up an old Jewish formula, the Fathers often explained that the treasure or the pearl was a charismatic understanding of Scripture, and that it was necessary to sacrifice all in order to acquire it.

"He sells what he has. He purchases the field, that is to say, scorning temporal things, he buys himself the necessary leisure for studying Scripture (the two Testaments, the treasure) and for becoming rich in the knowledge of God" (Augustine).

"Circling all around the field and scrutinizing the Scriptures and seeking to understand the Christ, he finds the treasure which is within himself; and having found it, he hides it, knowing that there is danger in revealing to the first person that comes along the secret thoughts of the Scriptures or the treasures of wisdom and of knowledge which are in the Christ. And having hidden it, he goes about completely preoccupied by the purchasing of the field; that is to say, of the Scriptures, in order to make it his personal property, receiving from God the words of God which at first had been confided to the Jews. And the disciples of the Christ having purchased the field, the kingdom of God is taken away from the former and is given to a new people who bear its fruits" (Origen).

"The Law and the Prophets are the good pearl which the merchant seeks. Listen to Marcion; listen to Mani: the good pearls are the Law and the Prophets and the learning of the Old Testament. But there is a pearl, precious above all: this is the knowledge of the Saviour and the mystery hidden in his Passion and his Resurrection. The merchant who discovers it, in imitation of St. Paul, scorns, as he would scavengers and shellfish, all the secrets of the Law and the Prophets. In comparison with that pearl, every other precious stone becomes contemptible" (St. Jerome).

"One must put preaching (the explanation of the Scriptures) above all, and with joy" (St. John Chrysostom).

The exegesis of St. Gregory the Great, the former prefect of Rome, who renounced silks and precious stones to give himself to poverty and obedience under the Rule of St. Benedict, is much closer to the letter of the Gospel. "The treasure is the desire for heaven; the field, the habit of studying the things of heaven. That man buys the field at the price of all his goods who renounces the pleasures of the flesh and crushes his earthly desires through observance of the heavenly rule (an observance which will bring life's peace and joy.)"

The saints' examples and the exhortations of the Fathers of the Church will be a source of great attraction for exuberant young people: that of all or nothing. One pretends to sell everything, and because

one has not the great courage—or the great grace—
necessary for total immediate renunciation, one does
nothing. This is identical to those travelers who have
prepared everything for a long expedition—furs for
braving the polar ice, and biscuits—and who never
leave. One will find the biscuits intact twenty years
later. "Man passes his entire life in front of the open
door. Why doesn't he enter? And what is absolutely
tragic is that he remains in front of the door, and
that he acts, in a sense, in good faith and out of good
will. For he could very well turn his back on the
door and leave to run around the country. But he
remains all his life before the door, and no one, not
even himself perhaps, will ever know why he did
not enter. However, God is not culpable, since he
has opened the door; and because one cannot force
man to go through it" (Lévy).

PART TWO

THE NEW JUSTICE

The Kingdom of God was henceforth present on earth in the Word of Jesus: in his person, in the little community he had founded, and in men's hearts. Its principles were so opposed to Jewish legalism that the just, according to the justice of the law, were no longer even disposed to a new "justice." If one still spoke the old language, one no longer understood it in the same way.

It was inevitable that the Pharisees take sides against Jesus. Between them and him, conflicts were numerous. His disciples, imitating him, stopped respecting the sterile laws of the sect. They observed neither the fasts nor the Sabbath rest. To the bitter-sweet remarks, Jesus retorted: "Surely the bridegroom's attendants would never think of mourning as long as the bridegroom is still with them?" (Matt. 9:15). "No one puts a piece of unshrunken cloth on to an old cloak. . . . Nor do people put new wine into old wineskins . . ." (Matt. 9:16f.). He takes exception to his mission: "It is not the healthy who need the doctor, but the sick" (Matt. 9:12). He takes the offensive: "If any one of you here had only one sheep and it fell down a hole on the Sabbath day, would he not get hold of it and lift it out?" (Matt. 12:11).

IV

THE MERCY OF GOD

The revelation of mercy seals the destiny of legalism. The latter had sapped all the strength of the Old Testament. Repeatedly Jesus reminded the Pharisees that their attitude contradicted the very essence of the religion: "Go and learn the meaning of the words: What I want is mercy, not sacrifice" (Matt. 9:13; 12:7).

Jesus thirsts only for the Fatherhood, the goodness, the mercy which are the basis of God's nature. Already in the Sermon on the Mount are sketched some parables: "Look at the birds in the sky. They do not sow or reap or gather into barns; yet your heavenly Father feeds them" (Matt. 6:26). "Think of the flowers growing in the fields; they never have to work or spin; yet I assure you that not even Solomon in all his regalia was robed like one of these. Now if that is how God clothes the grass in the field which is there today and thrown into the furnace tomorrow . . ." (Matt. 6:28-30).

Luke devotes a chapter of his Gospel to a trilogy of parables on the mercy of God. He introduces it: "The tax collectors and the sinners, meanwhile, were all seeking his [Jesus'] company to hear what he had to say, and the Pharisees and the scribes complained.

'This man' they said 'welcomes sinners and eats with them' " (Luke 15:1-2).

To welcome publicans and sinners, to seek out all the occasions for meeting them, is not the comportment of a pious man, and even less of someone who pretends to have received a religious mission from God. But precisely Jesus' mission explains his conduct. He reveals a new religious principle: God is good, merciful; men, all men, are his children. Jesus is good because he stands in God's place; it is in virtue of that that he discovers in sinners "lost" souls, those which God himself has lost, and for which he feels the loss: a father never ceases to be a father, whatever may be the ingratitude of his children.

The Good Shepherd (Luke 15:4-7)

At the period in which the trilogy places us, Jesus has not yet condemned the just of the old school; or rather—for he will never condemn them—he continues to believe that they will yet be able to listen to the Good News. The guardian of the sheep does not abandon the majority of the flock while he goes in search of a stray sheep. The flock is his flock, as Israel is always the people of God. But the moment has come to make room for the mangy sheep. These mangy sheep are precisely the privileged of God, for they need mercy. Upon mercy will be founded a new "justice," if not justice per se, that which is misunderstood by all the zealots of the Law: Pharisees, monks of Qumran, priests, and Levites of the Temple.

The first words of the parable are a call to the

hearts of those who refuse to understand Jesus; a
call also to the religious instinct that sleeps beneath
pharisaical prejudices: "What man among you with
a hundred sheep, losing one, would not leave the
ninety-nine in the wilderness and go after the missing
one till he found it?" We could easily reply that it is
imprudent to abandon the majority of the flock in
the wilderness. This is not in question. Already
Jesus is thinking of the application: the shepherd's
ways are those of heaven.

"And when he found it, would he not joyfully take
it on his shoulders . . .?" Without doubt, this is the
classic gesture of shepherds, but the gesture is stylized
to permit a glimpse of merciful love. How could
Jesus not have borne in mind the shepherd of Isaiah:
"He is like a shepherd feeding his flock, gathering
lambs in his arms, holding them against his breast
and leading to their rest the mother ewes" (Isa. 40:11).

All this in order to prepare for and validate the
point of the parable: "In the same way, I tell you,
there will be more rejoicing in heaven over one
repentant sinner than over ninety-nine virtuous men
who have no need of repentance."

The joy in heaven is God's joy. Or, rather, the
joy in the mystery of God, for it is better not to
speak of **his** joy. The modesty of a profoundly religious soul. The following parable will say: "the joy
among the angels of God."

By a game of arithmetical computation, the
Valentinian Gnostics demonstrated that the lost sheep

being the hundredth, with which the group of a hundred opens, was for that reason more precious than the ninety-nine, and represented the Gnostic. The Moslem tradition imparts this observation to Mohammed: God created a hundred portions of mercy; he reserved ninety-nine of them for himself, and left one of them for the world.

In the modern perception of the alienation of man, the problem is only to find faith in Christ again. This is the only solution, but it depends upon grace. The change of direction in existential philosophy brings us back to St. Hilary of Poitiers' exegesis: "By the one sheep we must understand man; and in the one man, we must see the totality. The human species is errant from the time it lost its way in Adam. . . . He who seeks out man, this is Christ; the lost man will again find the joy of heaven in him."

The Woman and the Lost Drachma (Luke 15:8-10)

We recognize a peasant's house, with its one, windowless room. As Jeremias proposes, were not the woman's ten drachmas her jewels?

The woman's zeal is unexpected; it is an "example." Truly it is a question of God's care for one sinner. One sinner who repents. We could say that all of Providence is suspended at that point in time and space when a sinner struggles to make his escape from the power of repentance which God has placed in his heart.

The Merciful Father (Luke 15:11-32)

The third parable takes on the aspect of an anecdote, of much freer style, into which Luke inserts, perhaps, something of himself—but without sinning against the law of fidelity to tradition, because for him who relates an anecdote, fidelity consists in embracing its flexibility. Under the veil of parable-allegory, Jesus reveals the extent of the divine mercy.

The eldest son, he who never transgressed one of his father's orders and who pretends to not have received all the recognition he "justly" expects as his reward, represents clearly enough the "just" of the old school. If one hesitates to make this identification, let him recall Matt. 21:28-32 (the first sketch, the design for the parable of the prodigal son): "A man had two sons . . . ." After having compared the conduct of the two sons—one who refuses to work, then is filled with remorse; and the other, who protests his obedience, but does not furnish the work expected —Jesus concludes: "I tell you solemnly, tax collectors and prostitutes are making their way into the kingdom of God before you." The evangelist remarks: "When they heard his parables, the chief priests and the scribes realized he was speaking about them" (Matt. 21:45).

The first and fundamental meaning of these three parables is the revelation of God's mercy. Their style differs visibly: which indicates that they were given under diverse circumstances. The parable of the drachma, literally speaking, is of the same popular and Galilean vein as the parable of the woman who prepares her bread, or of the woman who would cover the lamp with a bushel. The housewife has lost a drachma. The house is windowless, and dust covers the earthen floor on which is set rudimentary furniture. She lights the lamp, sweeps her house, searches carefully. The point is her childlike joy: exuberant, out of place for so small an experience. She assembles her friends and neighbors, and they improvise a party. The evangelist is right to draw the lesson: this woman's joy represents the joy of the angels of God over a sinner who repents.

The shepherd of the parable is none other than the one in Ezekiel, or in Deuteronomy; he is most particularly the one from Isaiah. He places the tired sheep on his shoulders. And like the woman with the drachma, he assembles friends and neighbors in order to rejoice.

The merciful father "was moved with pity" and his joy burst forth: "Quick! Bring out the best robe and put it on him; . . . Bring the calf we have been fattening, and kill it; we are going to have a feast, a celebration, because this son of mine was dead and has come back to life; he was lost and is found." This is the same point as in the first two parables, but a drama touches human souls to the quick.

V

THE JUST ACCORDING TO
THE HEART OF GOD

To the principle of God's mercy, which essentially is going to regulate the gift of salvation, corresponds a new human attitude replacing "justice according to the law." St. Paul designates this attitude as the "justice of God" or "justice by faith." Justice of God: this is a gift; justice by faith: man submits to God's gift by accepting it with confidence.

The parables of Jesus furnish the best proof there is of St. Paul's fidelity to Gospel doctrine. He did not invent justice by faith; he received it from Jesus and from the apostolic community. He inherited his reaction against legalism from the Galilean prophet. If he struggles for Christian liberty, Jesus, before him, had given his life for the same ideal.

To accept being the "creation" of God's mercy will be the new religious principle. Man no longer is content with rites and "sacrifices" of oxen and sheep, or with fasts, or with observances which meticulously fulfill the law. He will go **to the depths** of religion. He will know that God is so greatly above him that, in the depths of his being, the only attitude which suits him is to accept all and to owe everything.

Three of Luke's parables are built upon an identical scheme. Each of them sets in motion before God two antithetical roles. The merciful father must choose between his two sons: the prodigal or him who boasts of his fidelity. He chooses the prodigal. God loves the good Samaritan because, like himself, that man preferred mercy to sacrifices. He heard the Pharisee's prayer and the publican's, and justified the publican because of his confidence.

Jesus places on the scene personages held contemptible by Judaism: the public sinner, the Samaritan, the tax collector. New wineskins are necessary, and the old ones are cast into the refuse. The just according to the priestly or Pharisaic mode will play the bad part. They will play it naturally. Because of the very newness of the game, the Christian role will be entrusted to personages not committed to the law and until then scorned: in a single stroke the sinner, the Samaritan, the publican are rehabiltated— while waiting for the great conquest, the pagan. All just Christians will have to accept this role in order to know themselves. A Christian will be the prodigal son held up by the paternal shoulder; the "good Samaritan"; the publican at prayer.

The Prodigal Son (Luke 15:11-32)

Under a new title, we reread the parable of the "merciful father." The two titles suit the anecdote. Speaking truthfully, they should be reunited: the prodigal son becomes the repentant son, and at once he enters without difficulty into the father's love.

Rembrandt's genius admirably understood the profound intent of the story. The child remains in the shadows, kneeling, his back turned away from the viewer, his face buried in his father's breast. His tattered garments and his boots emerge from the shadows. The father's cloak is fully spread out, and all the light radiates from his face. The face of a venerable old man, his eyes dull from weeping, in which the energy of days gone by is no more than goodness grown tender. Trembling hands rest upon the shoulders of the young man, as if to hold him back. Another individual, standing in profile: the eldest son. Everything in his attitude is reproach for the father's weakness. The hairstyle underscores the narrowness of his brow. Eyebrows raised, lips drawn tight, and hands . . . those hands in which the repulsion of the entire body before the spectacle of the paternal disgrace ends in nervous contraction. From the shadows appear two servants, secondary personages, bantering.

Such is the "father" of the parable, made transparent by a mercy which comes from afar, from a higher source, and which illumines the entire scene. Can this be a different light from that possessed by the Father of mercy? The son's contrition will be itself a hymn to his goodness: "How many of my father's paid servants have more food than they want, and here am I dying of hunger! I will leave this place and go to my father . . . ."

But the son, for having uttered these words, "I will leave this place and go to my father," merits closer examination. To the father's mercy corresponds the son's attitude, which explains his "penitence." Unhappiness has broken his rebel heart. He already knows, before setting out, that he will find his father again. Mercy and repentance are two sides of a coin.

We know only too well the story of the younger son, raised in luxury. Having come of age, he requests his portion of the paternal inheritance. (He has this right: the eldest remains owner of the patrimony in joint tenancy with the father; the second son receives a third of the value of the estate.) The psychology of sin is the easiest psychology; one lets himself slide down the slope. The miracle is that when we are at the bottom of the abyss, an outstretched hand appears to raise us up.

Father Buzy placed the "Prodigal Son" of Puvis de Chavannes as the frontispiece of a work on the parables. Starving, his face drawn, his clothes in tatters, the rash young man tends the pigs. From the depths of his misery, he dreams of what will soon come to pass, when he will return to his father's home. He even prepares a little speech: "Father, I have sinned against heaven and against you; I no longer deserve to be called your son; . . ."[1] Confronted by the immense joy which heaved in his father's breast, he went no further.

They feasted in the father's house "Because this son of mine was dead and has come back to life; he was lost and is found." The eldest son came in from the fields. Refusing to enter, he cunningly questioned the servants. He became angry, sullen.

Before the old father's supplications, his countenance darkened more; mercy is being dealt with injustice: "Look, all these years I have slaved for you and never once disobeyed your orders, yet you never offered me so much as a kid for me to celebrate with my friends. But, for this son of yours, when he comes back after swallowing up your property—he and his women—you kill the calf we had been fattening." But the father allowed: "My son, you are with me always and all I have is yours. But it was only right we should celebrate and rejoice, because your brother here was dead and has come to life; he was lost and is found" (Luke 15:29-32).

It behooved St. Augustine to capture the theological profundity, almost "existential," of the parable. "The younger son left for a distant region, enjoying natural goods in an abusive manner, from the fact of having left his father, pushed by the desire to enjoy the flesh, abandoning the Creator. . . . Thus, the distant region is separation from God. The famine in that region is the absence of the word of truth." In our civilization we live intensely the drama of humanity. "Poor and great modern world: what a source of pride for this grandson of **pithecanthropus** to control atomic energy, to prepare to land on the moon, to attempt the synthesis of nucleic acids—the secret of life and of human thought—assured of the mastery of the physics and chemistry of the brain. Everything is possible" (P. Chauchard). The temptation is great for the modern prodigal son to abandon the paternal foyer of the old religions for the distant region. Nevertheless, it is the child that God always loves, whose return he awaits. The prodigal children, the multitude of humans—God knows them all by their name—those who despair in the distant region, "an absurd and incoherent world where ideologies seem powerless to free us from evil." He waits for them, one by one. Our role is to extend **his** hand to each one of those whose path we cross on the road of our return to the paternal house.

Let us dare to restate the words of Christian tradition, sure of the paternity of this God of mercy: "No one is a father like God" (Tertullian). Psichari comments: "I have been found," says God, "by those who did not seek me. I have shown myself to those who did not think of me. And it is I, O young soldier, who will take the first step. Humble submission, the taste for fidelity suffice me. I do not ask more of them. I will make you come from afar, and I will love you with my eternal love. I will mark you with the sign of my election. No more from them is necessary for me; truthfully, that imperceptible movement of an honest heart suffices me. Am I not the Father? And who can measure the tenderness of a father? A father, when he hears his child's mumblings, is amazed at his intelligence, and turns the least action into a reason for praising his child. I am that Father, and all those souls who are righteous and poor, and who are lonely and miserable, I am their Father and they are my chosen" (**Voyage,** pp. 80f.),

If there are still Christians who are scandalized to learn "that there will be more rejoicing in heaven

over one repentant sinner than over ninety-nine
virtuous men who have no need of repentance," let
us say to them again, in accord with tradition: the
virtuous men who have no need of repentance are
an inert species. The Pharisees were the "virtuous
men" of Our Lord's time. They have no need of
repentance. They feel no need to do penance. That
is what is terrible. Not to feel that one needs to do
penance, not to turn away from self with horror,
with contempt: that is to close oneself to God. That
is to refuse to be a creature, to refuse to be the
nothingness which God holds in his powerful hand
above the abyss which we "create" in our turn; to
exclude ourselves from participating in true justice—
the new relation to God which alone can renew man
in the depths of his being. Harboring a false attitude,
this is to reject mercy.

The Good Samaritan (Luke 10:29-37)

Luke locates the scene—which could recall a real
incident—on the road from Jerusalem to Jericho, a
long descent (16 and ¾ miles between Jerusalem and
Jericho) which is even today famous for attacks by
bandits (Jeremias). Jesus will follow the route in the
opposite direction at the time of his last pilgrimage.

The hero of the parable is a very ordinary man—
a traveler, who has only what is necessary for travel-
ing: his mule, and on its saddle his small baggage,
in which one would find a bottle of oil, a small jug
of wine, some strips of linen. The man is familiar
with the inns. For the rest, there is a Samaritan,

from a nation scarcely recommendable; and he is going down from Jerusalem, where he has not been to adore God. He prefers his mountain, Mount Gerizim, where the patriarchs sacrificed.

But under the mantle of a "common" traveler beats an uncommon heart. At a bend in the road, his mule rears. A man lies outstretched there, his face bloody, perhaps murdered. . . . In his throat is the death-rattle; the traveler approaches. He understands the crafty behavior of the two travelers who preceded him: a Jewish priest and a Levite. Just at this spot they turned their mules aside in order not to pass too close to a dead man, thus avoiding a defilement which could have upset their ritual order of the day.

The Samaritan does not share their scruples. He has compassion. "He went up and bandaged his wounds, pouring oil and wine on them" (a prescription of old Hippocrates). "He then lifted him on to his own mount . . . ," the merchant himself on foot and supporting the wounded man fraternally, ". . . carried him to the inn, and looked after him. Next day, he took out two denarii and handed them to the inn-keeper. 'Look after him,' he said 'and on my way back I will make good any extra expense you have.'"

That appears very simple—what this brave man did there. "Charity," said Péguy, "comes naturally. In order to love one's neighbor, one has only to let go; one has only to look at so much distress. For one not to love one's neighbor, it would be necessary that he do violence to himself, to torture himself, to torment himself, to thwart himself. To harden himself. To hurt himself. To pervert himself. To live unnaturally; to go backwards. Then to arise again, changed. Charity is completely natural, completely spontaneous, completely simple, easily come by. It is the first movement of the heart. It is the first movement which is good. Charity is a mother and a sister."

Without doubt, it is very simple to be "human" (in the connotation that a Christian civilization has imposed on the word). But it is not to that, that the parable leads us. One thing makes us shudder: the Jewish priest, the Jewish Levite, from their religion, conjured up only reasons to excuse them from pity. A Pharisee would extol them for having placed care for legal purity above charity. The Samaritan, even if he had to overcome his disgust in order to pick up the bloody dying man from the side of the road, if he himself, a Samaritan, succored a Jew (the man, spent his money on the victim (was he so rich?), if he himself, (a Samaritan, succored a Jew (the parable, moreover, does not tell us that the dying man was a Jew), it is for another reason that Jesus gives him to us as an example: his charity is a religious act which henceforth will be understood as the basis for holiness.

The old commentary of Bruce explained: "The moral of this story is that charity is true holiness. It is the key to the entire structure of the parable. More particularly, that explains to us the choice of personages: a priest and a Levite (holy people by profession and occupation) and a Samaritan stranger, from another race than the man who had need of his neighbor's help. The first two accentuate the parable's lesson through the contrast which they suggest between true holiness (out of love) and degenerate forms of holiness; the last man, through his good deed, puts in relief the supreme value of love in God's eyes. Our parable is emphatically a parable of grace; it reveals to us the nature of God and of his kingdom."

It was the old religion that spoke through the mouth of the scribe when he posed the unique question to Jesus: " 'Master, what have I to do to inherit eternal life?'—what does the Law say?—You shall love the Lord your God with all your heart, with all your soul, and with all your might and your neighbor as yourself.—A good answer. Do likewise and you shall live." He had to be content with that. But the scribe insists: "Who is my neighbor?" He had never understood the profound religious principle which unites, identifies almost all love of God and love of neighbor: "He who does not love all men loves none of them as a neighbor; for a neighbor is a fraternal being, and we are all brothers in God. To exclude a man from this communion is to exclude God, and to exclude God is to exclude all fraternal connexion" (Sertillanges). If God is mercy, how could he who loves him not be all merciful. "Be merciful, as your Father is merciful" (Luke 6:36).

The Fathers unanimously explained the parable as a mystery: "It is all of wounded humanity that lies at the side of the road in the person of the man whom the thieves—the devil and his angels," St. Augustine says brutally, "—robbed." When a man, in charity, bends down toward this humanity, whether he touches his soul or his spirit or his body, it is always Jesus, the good Samaritan, who stoops. A gesture of true charity becomes Christ's gesture, up to Christ's standard, for all of humanity.

We cannot refrain from calling to mind the immensity of the charitable treasures dispensed by all our human brothers. How many admirable actions are there, under Christ's prompting, which save the world? The agonizing problem, moreover, resolves itself easily in our societies which are profoundly impregnated by Christianity. Charity, by multiple channels, descends from the Church and the people have reason to speak, in this respect, of good Samaritans. It is Christ to whom their altruism is addressed (Matt. 25:40). But does not the charity of those who have not been touched by Christian revelation also come forth from the Christian soul—Christian at least by destination and creation? It is so simple for God, Creator and Savior, in the very moment when his creature surpasses himself by helping his neighbor, to cover him again with the mantle of Christ.

The ancients had a presentiment of that extraordinary order of salvation in their theories concerning the Word and the Gospel preparation; and those theories are still applicable to contemporary humanity. The divine clairvoyance from the Judge's countenance on the last day will discover the religious quality of the actions in which man renounced self for someone beyond himself.

A hope, like steam from hot, moist earth, rises from the mystery of charity. "Go and do likewise," the scribe heard. "Thus with that word," notes Leenhardt in an exegesis which he calls **existentialist,** "we see opening the perspective of the new times, during which God makes new things and new men. For that man, Jesus' word strikes the hour for this renewal. There is a Good News for repentant hearts; there is a tomorrow for those who have ceased to cling to their past. When man stops wishing to build upon himself, God sovereignly intervenes. Jesus, through his word, created a new tomorrow for that man; he introduced him to a new life. With the word of Jesus, eternity enters into the history of this Pharisee."

May God, in his mercy and his mystery, render Jesus present to all the souls of good will who, believing not to know him, encounter him through charity.

A fear spreads over us also when we notice the egoism of our lives. "When the Son of Man comes in his glory, escorted by all the angels, then he will take his seat on his throne of glory. All the nations will be assembled before him and he will separate men one from another as the shepherd separates sheep from goats. . . . Then the King will say to those on his right hand, 'Come, you whom my Father has blessed, take for your heritage the kingdom prepared

for you since the foundation of the world. For I was
hungry and you gave me food; I was thirsty and you
gave me drink; I was a stranger and you made me
welcome; naked and you clothed me, sick and you
visited me, in prison and you came to see me'" (Matt.
25:31-36).

All of Christian civilization is born in this parable.
Have we still today the courage and the illumination
to begin anew this miracle of grace?

The Prayer of the Publican (Luke 18:9-14)

The parable is clearly directed against the Pharisees. Its picturesque and realistic qualities, very lifelike as regards Palestinian customs, the inimitable
sense of true prayer (diametrically opposed to legalism) assure us of its authenticity. It is even so stylis-
tically. "There is no other parable in Luke in which
the Semitic asyndeton (vv. 11, 12, 14) is so frequent;
the language and the content prove, moreover, that
we have here an old Palestinian tradition" (Jeremias).

Luke begins: "He spoke the following parable to
some people who prided themselves on being virtuous
and despised everyone else" (18:9). One obviously
recognizes the Pharisees who multiply devotional
practices: prayers, fasts, almsgiving, reading of the
law (especially reading of the law, which remits sins
and makes saints. The monks of Qumran esteemed it
more.) It is not these devotions which improve one.
God does not find love there; men do not find goodness.

From the heights of their justice, the Pharisees

scorn "the others." These others: the publicans, coarse Jews. Sociologically, these are the assessors, the tax collectors, in the service of the Romans or the Herods. Religiously, they were not concerned with the Pharisees' rules of piety; they did not wash a hundred times a day; they did not wash the vegetables they bought in the market. They were always impure. Other than this, they were not necessarily believers.

Two men went up to the Temple at the hour of prayer—it may have been nine o'clock in the morning or three o'clock in the afternoon. Standing, his back rigid, the Pharisee prayed thus, steeped in self-esteem: "I thank you, God, that I am not grasping, unjust, adulterous like the rest of mankind, and particularly that I am not like this tax collector here. I fast twice a week; I pay tithes on all I get." As for the publican, he did not pass beyond the threshold of the outer courtyard. He dared not even raise his eyes to heaven, and he beat his breast, saying: "God, be merciful to me, a sinner."

"This man, I tell you, went home again at rights with God." Because he knew how to pray. "When you pray, do not imitate the hypocrites: they love to say their prayers standing up in the synagogues and at the street corners for people to see them. I tell you solemnly, they have had their reward. But when you pray, go to your private room and, when you have shut your door, pray to your Father who is in that secret place . . ." (Matt. 6:5-6).

The contrast between the two prayers is that of the two fundamental attitudes in religion. One re-

mains on the plane of pride, the other is humility.
Pride or humility molds souls.

The Pharisee takes a position opposite God. He
is "standing." This is, it is true, the prescribed attitude. Thus Maimonides, the great Jewish theologian:
Let no one pray unless he can remain standing. Certain Rabbis stated precisely: the legs straight, because
it is said in Ezekiel (1:7) concerning the animals who
carry the throne: "Their legs were straight." They
said "stand up" to pray as we say "kneel."

Standing or kneeling, only reverence counts. The
ancients were more ceremonious than we, and gave
more importance to etiquette. Our Pharisee, standing,
behaved on equal terms with God. Simon the
Magician had himself called the **Hestos** and this was,
in his thinking, an affirmation of divinity. God is
not a partner. A creature is not his equal.

Greek religion had an innate sense of the inequality between the gods and men. The immortals
are happy. A happy man disturbs them. Too great
happiness is an excess, an insolence toward them;
while unhappiness keeps us in our human place. The
suppliant is ennobled. Such is the spectacle in front
of Oedipus' palace at Thebes: the king, whom his
insolent happiness condemns, addresses himself to
the chorus: "Children, young posterity of ancient
Cadmos, why then are you thus on your knees, with
branches of supplication crowned with bandelets?"
The suppliants have the easy role.

We know better what God is, his infinite majesty—

which must nevertheless be kept close and paternal—
and we know that there is an infinite usurpation in
pride. Not that God wishes to exalt himself at the
cost of our abasement. If he loves that which is not,
it is in order to be able to make it what it might be.
If he loves him who knows that he is nothing, it is
because to know that one is nothing is the unique
means for becoming something with his help. Father
Sertillanges translated exactly St. Paul's thought:
"God's power in us is fashioned exactly from our
weakness, and the being of God in us from our own
nonexistence."

Prayer knows only two poles: the majesty of God
and the nothingness of man. The Pharisee knew only
of two others: self-esteem and scorn for others. His
prayer: "I thank you, God, that I am not . . . like the
rest of mankind," is not invented. We have preserved
a talmudic prayer from about the year A.D. 70,
attributed, if I am not mistaken, to Rabbi Nechonias
and which Jeremias translates as follows: "I thank
you, O Lord my God, for having given me a place
with those who sit in the house of teaching and not
with those who sit on street corners; for like them I
am going forward. But I am going quickly towards
the Word of the Law, and they are going quickly
towards futility. I work hard, they also; I work hard
and receive my reward, and they work hard but receive no reward. I run and they run. I run towards
the life of the next world, and they run towards the
pit of perdition."

Indeed, one should thank God for his favors. Because He gives them, but not because one possesses them. The benefits possessed become the object of conceit and pride.

Perhaps the Pharisee is not grasping, unjust, adulterous. But he omits certain imperfections in his life, and St. Paul, who had been a member of the group, had no great illusions about himself. In any case, if he had avoided sins, it is to God that he owed it; and if God abandoned him, he would be a criminal. We can convince ourselves of one value when we ascertain our baseness and our perfidy.

It is true that the Pharisee fasts and tithes. But is it worthwhile speaking about it? To fast: a trifling matter. People who play sports fast. We fast to lose weight. That does not make for human greatness in God's eyes. He gives a tenth of his goods. But players of casino give their entire fortune in one night.

To the infantile or malignant, esteem of self corresponds to scorn for others—thieves, unchaste men, like this publican. What do we know of our neighbor? We judge so quickly. The publicans are not very particular, certainly, but there are exceptions. And then: intentions and the divine plan. God reserves certain souls for himself, and their failures are preparations. Saul of Tarsus was a sinner. St. Augustine was a sinner. And Mary Magdalene. And so many others. God pursued them out of his love. He loved them for what they would be, for what he would make of them, for his magnificent gifts which he would place in them. Mud cleans precious metals.

Jesus so strongly condemned the critics that we should, once and for all, avoid being critics. A good practical rule: speak no evil until there is no more good to speak. Truthfully, all that has nothing to do with prayer. The mixing of prayer with vanity and criticism is against nature. Prayer is the splendor of union with God, not a mask behind which one continues to lead a banal, ordinary, indefinite life.

The Rule of St. Benedict copies its twelfth degree of humility from the Gospel portrait of the publican: "head always bent, gaze fixed on the ground . . . telling oneself ceaselessly in his heart what the publican of the Gospel says, his eyes rooted to the ground: Lord I am not worthy, I, a sinner, to raise my eyes to heaven." Bent, such as he appears on the mosaic of St. Apollinaris Nuovo at Ravenna, the publican brings to mind the priest at the foot of the altar during the Confiteor of the Mass. The weight of our sins and of those of the Christian people is heavy to bear. It is better to hide our face, filled as it is with confusion. The inner attitude replies to the outer: "God, be merciful to me, a sinner." St. Francis of Assisi paraphrased: "Who are you, O my God, and what am I, miserable earthworm!" To the nothingness of the creature, one adds the nothingness of the sin; and it is well thus for the creature. The saints said that, and they thought it! They thought it and they had reason to think it, for God's light made them understand their misery, which was true. They were only miserable men, bearers of a holiness which did not succeed in purifying their depths. For one

who thinks in this way, the action of grace has lost
its danger.

A true and beautiful working of grace is that
found in the Letter of St. Clement of Rome: "Thus
may the body that we form in Christ be entirely in
a good state, and may each one be submissive to
his neighbor according to the grace which has been
given him. May the strong man protect the weak;
may the weak man respect the strong. May the
rich man succor the poor; may the poor man render
thanks to God, who has given him what makes up
for his lack. May the wise man show his wisdom,
not in words, but in good works. May the humble
man not bear witness to himself, but wait for the
approbation of others. May he who is chaste in body
not glorify himself, knowing that it is another who
has given him the grace of continence. Thus let us
meditate, my brothers, upon the matter from which
we are born, who we are, and in what state we have
arrived in the world; upon what tomb and what
shadows he who has formed and created us has
introduced into his universe, after having prepared
his benefits for us before our birth. Possessing, thus,
all things from him, we must give thanks for all.
To him be glory throughout all ages of ages. Amen."

The publican does not detail his confession. The
Pharisee has made his confession for him. "One can,
therefore, without fear of erring, and if God directs
a spiritual life in this path, cling less to examinations
of conscience than to the loving prostration of the
entire being before the Creator: that love which loses

itself in the joyous and laudatory recognition of the divine perfections" (Gauthier). On condition that this method costs; that it consumes the "I." "It is by introspection that one makes the soul grow, as a plant grows in sunlight. But it is not upon oneself that this introspection should be cast; it is upon God within the self" (Sertillanges). On condition also that the individual conscience accepts the law of obedience to God and to the Church and that, in his thoughts and actions, the Christian of our day, in place of submitting to the attraction and the yoke of the "world," remains "the strong and austere disciple of Christ"—thus have all the popes after St. Clement continued to define him.

"This man, I tell you, went home again **justified;** the other did not." The use of this word is cruel. To be "justified" was the pride of the Pharisees. Jesus bestows it on the publicans: "For everyone who exalts himself will be humbled, but the man who humbles himself will be exalted."

Some exegetes maintain that the use of the verb "justify" in this parable does not come under Pauline influence. But Luke is not without having noticed that the Pauline doctrine of justification finds its strength in the thought of Jesus. True "justification" does not result from a rite or from "works," but from a gift of God responding to the attitude of humility and total confidence of the creature.

[1]". . . treat me as one of your paid servants." When he saw his father hastening toward him, he began the prepared speech: "Father, I have sinned against heaven and against you, I no longer deserve to be called your son."

VI

THE BREAK

The obstinacy of the Jewish authorities—Pharisees, doctors of the law, functionaries of the Temple—could only lead to the establishment of a new religious regime, in which the followers of Christ would take the place abandoned by the Jews. The prophetic tidings of the Old Testament were being fulfilled: "And every tree of the field will learn that I, Yahweh, am the one who stunts tall trees and makes the low ones grow . . ." (Ezek. 17:24; 21:31).

Jesus returns to the prophet's proverb. He places it at the conclusion of the parable of the Pharisee and the publican: "For everyone who exalts himself will be humbled, but the man who humbles himself will be exalted." We find it again as a finale to a parable of the wedding feast in Luke 14:11. Matthew introduces it in his discourse against the scribes and Pharisees, 23:12. It is even the basis for Christian justice, which Paul explains in another manner by the words of Jeremiah: "If anyone wants to boast, let him boast about the Lord" (Jer. 9:22; 1 Cor. 1:31; 2 Cor. 10:17; cf. Gal. 6:14).

The Children Playing in the Market Place
(Matt. 11:16-19; Luke 7:31-35)

The parable starts with a familiar scene. Children

play in the market place; the boys propose a wedding, the girls a funeral.

"What description can I find for this generation? It is like children shouting to each other as they sit in the market place:

> We played the pipes for you,
> and you wouldn't dance;
> we sang dirges,
> and you wouldn't be mourners.

"For John (the Baptist) came, neither eating nor drinking, and they say, 'He is possessed.' The Son of Man came, eating and drinking, and they say, 'Look, a glutton and a drunkard, a friend of tax collectors and sinners.' Yet wisdom has been proved right by her actions."

The style cries out with truth. Tradition has not even obscured the insults addressed to Christ: it has preserved them, through care for faithfully reproducing memories. The final phrase, in which Matthew's version (". . . by her actions") is preferable to Luke's (". . . by all her children") is explained by Luke 7:30: "The Pharisees and the lawyers had thwarted what God had in mind for them."

The Jewish authorities contemporary with Christ refused God's message; they cut themselves off from the plan of salvation. Only a small portion of the people, the least interesting for the Pharisees (since publicans and sinners abound there) continued to believe in the Good News. In this sense we can speak of a break. Responsibility for it was incumbent upon the official authorities, the Pharisees and the lawmakers.

The Two Sons (Matt. 21:28-32)

Matthew has brought together three parables involving a break: the two sons, the wicked husbandmen, and the wedding feast. At the beginning of this combination, which goes back without doubt to Aramaic tradition, he indicates to us the occasion for it (Matt. 21:23-27). Jesus, in Jerusalem, was grappling with the Jewish authorities who demanded proof of the divine authority of which he was making use. He diverts the question to John the Baptist: Whence proceeded this man's mandate? If it came from God, why had not the Jewish authorities followed it? Here is the first parable.

"What is your opinion? A man had two sons. He went and said to the first, 'My boy, you go and work in the vineyard today.' He answered, 'I will not go,' but afterwards thought better of it and went. The man then went and said the same thing to the second who answered, 'Certainly, sir,' but did not go. Which of the two did the father's will? 'The first' they said. Jesus said to them, 'I tell you solemnly, tax collectors and prostitutes are making their way into the kingdom of God before you. For John came to you, a pattern of true righteousness, but you did not believe him, and yet the tax collectors and prostitutes did. Even after seeing that, you refused to think better of it and believe in him.' "

By reason of its intention and its controversial

character, this parable is parallel to that of the children who play in the market place. Jesus has nothing more to be careful of. To the publicans who were a source of example for the Pharisees, Matthew this time joins the prostitutes. We are in Jesus' last days in Jerusalem, at the time when his death—he knew it—was decided by the authorities.

The controversial atmosphere, the direct and popular style, the recalling of the Baptist's mission, which ran aground like that of Jesus', are common to the two parables. On both sides, it is a question of a true "parable" without any intention, at least in the particulars, of allegorization. The introduction is familiar. Instead of saying "son" Jesus says "child."[1] The dialogue is very lifelike. Of the two sons, one is hotheaded and goodhearted; the other is obsequious, very respectful, but a malingerer. The father has reasons to distrust the latter.

The chief priests and the elders are caught in a trap by Jesus' question. They have not understood the lesson. They have seen publicans and women of the street believe in the Baptist and be restored to a better life, and they remained shut up in their idolatry of the law.

The misunderstanding concerning the work of the vineyard (the Kingdom of God), is deep between Jesus—also John—and the authorities of Judaism. There is a religious piece of work which is not God's —which seems to correspond to his will, but which does not know the true scope of the divine demands.

Parable of the Wicked Husbandmen
(Matt. 21:33-46; Mark 12:1-12; Luke 20:9-19)

The refusal to receive the message, the incomprehension of the Jews before the "sign of the times" takes on, in Jesus' eyes, its full meaning: those whom, from the beginning, he called to the kingdom—the poor, then the sinners, the tax collectors, the Samaritans—henceforth constitute the only privileged group.

The three Synoptics concur in considering the parable of the wicked husbandmen as a prophetic farewell made by Jesus to the Jewish people. At the same time a vision of the future is afforded: the vineyard will be given to more honest husbandmen. Jesus, the stone rejected by the builders, will become the cornerstone of a new edifice. The differences between the three evangelists are of no consequence. Luke, according to his custom, copies Mark. He abridges the quotation from Isaiah to which Jesus has reference, but the phrase "he planted a vineyard" suffices to indicate it. He quotes only in part the text of Ps. 118:22f.; in return, he comments on it. In the three, the parable unfolds between the text of Isa. 5:2 and the psalm; the latter will be taken up again by Peter, Acts 4:11 and 1 Pet. 2:7.

There is nothing in Jesus' utilization of texts from the Old Testament to surprise us, particularly not in the presence of those cited above. The song of the vineyard, unforgettable for whoever has heard and understood it, recapitulates the entire mission of the great prophets. Is there a valid objection to the use

of Ps. 118 in Acts with respect to the resurrection?
It was very necessary that someone first notice a
word so expressive of the history of the Christian
movement. The "construction" image is familiar to
Jesus. "In short," concludes V. Taylor, "it is more
probable that the interest which primitive Christianity
took in Christ's idea—stone rejected by men, but made
by God the cornerstone of a new Temple—is based
on tradition; and that Jesus himself made use of
Ps. 118:22f. in a scathing attack upon the Jewish
hierarchy."

We will take as our basic text that of Luke, because it is the most concise.

"A man planted a vineyard and leased it to
tenants, and went abroad for a long while. When
the time came, he sent a servant to the tenants to
get his share of the produce of the vineyard from
them. But the tenants thrashed him, and sent him
away empty-handed. But he persevered and sent a
second servant; they thrashed him too and treated
him shamefully and sent him away empty-handed.
He still persevered and sent a third; they wounded
this one also, and threw him out. Then the owner
of the vineyard said, 'What am I to do? I will send
them my dear son. Perhaps they will respect him.'
But when the tenants saw him they put their heads
together. 'This is the heir,' they said 'let us kill him
so that the inheritance will be ours.' So they threw
him out of the vineyard and killed him.

" 'Now what will the owner of the vineyard do to
them? He will come and make an end of these

tenants and give the vineyard to others.' Hearing this they said, 'God forbid!' But he looked hard at them and said, 'Then what does this text in the Scriptures mean: It was the stone rejected by the builders that became the keystone?' "

Great has been the temptation for the Fathers to seek in this parable a detailed history of the people of God, and to read there his reprobation. Irenaeus expands the horizon: "God planted the vineyard of humankind by the creation of Adam and the appointment of the Patriarchs; he transmitted it to the husbandmen by that Law which was given through Moses . . . ." Origen, basing himself upon Matt. 2:43, sees in the vineyard the doctrine of the Scriptures united to the contemplation of God; the mysteries of the Scripture belong henceforth to the Christians. This is St. Paul's formula.

The character of the parable and its circumstances impose a certain amount of allegory. The parable encloses itself naturally in a polemical dialogue. Jesus takes the offensive against the Pharisees and doctors of the law. The parable is aimed at them; it describes, under a transparent veil, their dramatic situation. Why should certain features not be construed as allegory? That the Gospel tradition underscored them is normal. Is the fact that they are missing in the Gospel of Thomas a peremptory argument for rejecting them? Even if this apocryphal writer had some chance of representing an original tradition in certain aspects, his perpetual Gnostic allegorizing dissuaded him from preserving the reasoning of our Synoptics. At the moment when all appears lost, Jesus envisages the future of his work. The refusal of the Jews is accomplished; Judaism (taken as an aggregate), inseparable from its leaders, will not accept the last prophetic effort. It will not deny its glorious past for a future of mystery. It will not renounce its position as the Chosen People in order to accept a religious framework in which its privileges threaten to be disregarded, its law scorned, the Temple, its sacrifices, its priesthood replaced by a worship from within. God will draw the inferences.

Jesus' parable-allegory, his testament and at the same time his final protestation against legalistic Judaism, is sketched upon a very simple canvas, which continues the allegory of the vineyard in Isaiah. The husbandmen, absent in Isaiah, appear: but were they not already there, responsible for the unfruitfulness of the vineyard? It is from them that God demands the fruits. Moreover, was not the punishment for Isaiah's vineyard meted out to its husbandmen? The song closes with a mysterious promise for the future. Jesus transposes it onto his horizon. The vineyard is at the same time the Israel of God, the Kingdom, and the true justice which God demands. People, Kingdom, justice will have to pass into a new order, that one which Jesus is beginning on earth with all those who listen to him.

The parable's call is pathetic—at that moment when Jesus is rejected by those to whom he wished to open the treasures of the Kingdom of heaven. The husbandmen have gone to the limit of their malice.

They are treating the last messenger of the Kingdom as they have treated the prophets. The evils which the latter proclaimed are going to pounce upon Jerusalem, which has not heard God's last call. But the call is the Word of God; it does not fall in vain. Who will hear it? No one is excluded. No one is absolutely privileged. Are the Christians of today? The call is eminently personal, and the response is personal. The parable condemned definitively the false security of the doctors of the law and the priests. No security exists any more outside of confidence in the work of God.

Have we noticed that the parable does not determine the portion that returns to the proprietor? This is because the proprietor is God, who intends to demand the totality of his vineyard's fruit. Every man is his vineyard, according to Jesus' doctrine. The totality of lives belongs to him. Man will no longer be in command of anything, in order to be totally free for the future which opens before him. The Jews walled themselves up in their legalism, their "practices" of piety, their sacrifices, their liturgy. They themselves had decreed that God's call could no longer pass through this framework. We, ourselves, are also formed by our Christian centuries and our contemporary culture. We know that tithes do not suffice, nor the "hours" of prayer, nor fasts; that all of that does not exhaust the call. God's voice is more imperious, more totalitarian; so austere, also, that there remains for us only one recourse for escaping it: the noise of the world. If at least we still know that from it proceeds the harmony of the spheres!

The Great Feast (Matt. 22:1-14; Luke 14:16-24)

We arrive at a parable found in two rather different versions. In Matthew the "wedding feast" follows, and for general purposes is equivalent to, the parable of the wicked husbandmen. The atmosphere remains that of the last days in Jerusalem and of the decisive moment. Jesus draws the lesson from his losses, with the certitude that God's work is being done, and will be achieved in spite of human contradictions. Let us listen first to Matthew's narrative.

"The kingdom of heaven may be compared to a king who gave a feast for his son's wedding. He sent his servants to call those who had been invited, but they would not come. Next he sent some more servants. 'Tell those who have been invited' he said 'that I have my banquet all prepared, my oxen and fattened cattle have been slaughtered, everything is ready. Come to the wedding.' But they were not interested: one went off to his farm, another to his business, and the rest seized his servants, maltreated them and killed them. The king was furious. He dispatched his troops, destroyed those murderers and burnt their town. Then he said to his servants, 'The wedding is ready; but as those who were invited proved to be unworthy, go to the crossroads in the town and invite everyone you can find to the wedding.' So these servants went out on to the roads and collected together everyone they could find, bad and good alike; and the wedding hall was filled with guests."

Luke's version will permit us to "criticize" Matthew's. Luke inserts the parable in a section entitled the "Banquet" (the well-known old Greek literary form). The exclamation of a guest serves to introduce it: "Happy the man who will be at the feast in the kingdom of God!" Thus one expects a parable of the Kingdom, in which Luke will seek to preserve the allure of an intimate conversation.

"There was a man who gave a great banquet, and he invited a large number of people. When the time for the banquet came, he sent his servant to say to those who had been invited, 'Come along: everything is ready now.' But all alike started to make excuses. The first said, 'I have bought a piece of land and must go and see it. Please accept my apologies.' Another said, 'I have bought five yoke of oxen and am on my way to try them out. Please accept my apologies.' Yet another said, 'I have just got married and so am unable to come.'

"The servant returned and reported this to his master. Then the householder, in a rage, said to his servant, 'Go out quickly into the streets and alleys of the town and bring in here the poor, the crippled, the blind and the lame.' 'Sir,' said the servant 'your orders have been carried out and there is still room.' Then the master said to his servant, 'Go to the open roads and the hedgerows and force people to come in to make sure my house is full; because, I tell you, not one of those who were invited shall have a taste of my banquet.'"

Incidentally, the Palestinian Talmud recounts for us an analogous story. The rich tax collector Bar

Majan had organized a great feast for the important people of his borough. They refused the invitation. Then rather than see it spoil, he made the poor come to eat his repast. But Luke does not stop at a little story. The introduction indicates that the narrative has reference, in one manner or another, to the Kingdom of God, and the final allusion to punishment by exclusion from the feast makes every good listener think about the messianic feast. The places of the first invited are definitely occupied by newcomers. We are back at the ending of the parable of the vine-dresser.

At first sight, the actual conclusion of the parable in Matt. 22:11-14 introduces the idea of the eschatological judgment: "When the king came in to look at the guests he noticed one man who was not wearing a wedding garment, and said to him, 'How did you get in here, my friend, without a wedding garment?' And the man was silent. Then the king said to the attendants, 'Bind him hand and foot and throw him out into the dark, where there will be weeping and grinding of teeth.' For many are called, but few are chosen."

Some commentators consider that Matthew has joined two distinct parables: that of the feast to which are invited last-minute guests, and that of the examination of the guests, concluded by eschatological punishment. We know, however, that the messianic feast (representing, in fact, the Church on earth already enjoying, in mystery, the eternal joys) is easily transformed into the eschatological feast (directly envisaging eternity) which is, as well in Jesus' thought as in that of the evangelists, according to the natural propensity of the Jewish milieu.

The Fathers well understood the parable of the feast. St. Augustine furnishes us with a brief commentary on it, distinguishing by a historical and moral application the diverse categories of guests. "All those mendicants arriving from the town," he writes, "those are the Jews, sinners, tax collectors, etc., weakened by their sins, happily not having that pride found in the false Pharisaic justice, the insurmountable obstacle which prevents the chosen from receiving God's gift. As for the others," he adds, "whom the king orders to be brought from the hedgerows and the open roads, these are the pagans, entangled in their philosophical and religious sects and in the nettle of their sins."

Can one truly hold a grievance against this exegesis for being based upon an allegorical signification? Jesus, however, had insight into the destinies of his human work. Was his message to stop at the frontiers of the Jewish world?

The People Who Produce Its Fruit (Matt. 21:43)

Matthew, in concluding the parable of the husbandmen, sketches another parable, aiming at the Christian future: "I tell you, then, that the kingdom of God will be taken from you and given to a people who will produce its fruit." In this "people" everyone recognizes the Church. (The style is not Matthew's, as the expression "kingdom of God," unusual in him, shows. This is no reason for rejecting the authenticity of a very ancient logion.)

Jesus never doubted concerning the future of his message. Why would he doubt it when facing the prospect of his death? But if his work, that is to say the Kingdom founded upon earth, was to endure, is it not in the gathering to himself of the subjects who will replace the Jews? Jesus' prophecy (for this vision of the future is that of a prophet, because the survival of a "remainder," of a "stock," after the punishment of the Jewish nation, is a theme eminently prophetic) does nothing but explain precisely what the parables of the break announced symbolically. The latter already place against the incredulity of the Jewish authorities the fidelity of the husbandmen who render to the master of the vineyard the tribute which by nature is due to him, or the good will of the last-minute guests. From the time of the parable of the darnel and of the dragnet until that of the workers at the last hour, the idea of a temporal period belonging to the history of the Kingdom comes to light in Jesus' teaching. The good and the bad wait together for the yet unknown hour of the settling of accounts before God.

The traditional images bring to mind the Church. We could reconsider in this light the parables of the mustard seed and the leaven, and in general the parables of growth. The entire reality of the Church is already present in this Kingdom, which begins in secret and to which is promised a glorious destiny.

Two images predominate: that of the flock and

that of the vineyard. They are solidly rooted in the Old Testament. From time immemorial, flocks of sheep and goats were part of the Palestinian landscape. The good shepherd of the prophets has scarcely changed his appearance in becoming the one in Luke 15:3-7. From the little band which the disciples form (Luke 12:32) combined with Zech. 13:7 (cf. Mark 14:27; Matt. 26:31) comes a moving parable about the destiny of the Church. And Jesus, identifying with the shepherd in Zechariah, the parable becomes an allegory. The allegory unfolds in another direction when the theme of the lost sheep is applied to the leaders of the community in Matt. 18:12-14. John's Gospel brings back the same allegory of the flock under all its aspects (John 10:1-16, 26-28; cf. 21:15-17). As to the allegory of the vine-dresser in the Synoptic tradition, it becomes deeper in a mystical sense in "the true vine" of the same Gospel (15:1-8); this sense will pass into the liturgy of the Didache: "We thank you, our Father, for the holy vine of David, your servant, which you have revealed in Jesus, your Servant . . ." (Did. 9:3), clearly manifesting the unity of the divine work accomplished by the glorification of the Creator in Jesus' humanity.

[1]In the French text quoted by the author.

PART THREE

THE ETERNAL HARVEST

The parables of the Kingdom terminate on the perspective of its eschatological blossoming. The planting makes ready the harvest. It has no purpose in being except for "the full grain in the ear." Contrasted with the mustard seed, the great tree marks the glorious phase of the Kingdom: Jesus thinks of the present time in terms of a heavenly fullness.

One can say, if one wishes, that **eschatology is realized** in the Kingdom of heaven present upon earth. But the realization is secret and mysterious, and the actual Kingdom remains always "eschatology." Having come from God, it tends toward eschatological fullness, for it has received its worth from that. That which is sown in time is eternity. That which grows and matures is a reality of eternity already mysteriously present in our temporal lives.

The hour of the harvest will unavoidably sound at the moment of the divine decision. We must take Jesus' words seriously: "But as for that day and hour, nobody knows it, neither the angels of heaven, nor the Son, no one but the Father only" (Matt. 24:36). All comes to rest both in the ignorance of the hour and in the certitude of an ending; the human race, its successive generations, individual human lives—all terminate in that certitude which hangs over life and which will determine everything. At the hour of the harvest these lives will enter into eternity.

With reference to the unavoidable hour, our duration of time loses its absolute value. The encounter with the Kingdom is the only human adventure which counts.

Between the planting and the hour of the harvest flows a temporal continuance. Short or long? No one can know that, since its end, the hour of the harvest, is an unknown. The prospect of Jesus' "return" awakens the hope that the duration will be brief. In the parables of the planting, nothing stops the growth: one must await maturity, and that state is as completely certain as growth. This is all that one can guarantee: "When the wheat is ripe, one begins to reap."

VII

THE JUDGMENT OF GOD

When one reflects on this intermediate period of time and when one establishes undeniably that God permits men their liberty, whether to do good or evil, one is led, in line with the Old Testament, to think of a judgment. The hour of the harvest is also that of the judgment found in Jewish tradition.

The Word of God is the power that nothing stops, and which fecundates the earth; but the darnel sprouts at the side of the good grain, in the same field. At the harvest hour, they will gather the good grain into the barn, and the darnel will be cast into the fire. This is the separation of the good and the bad: in Jewish idiom, the judgment. Thus the parables of planting are normally accompanied by the idea of a judgment between the earthly development of the Kingdom and its final celestial blossoming. Jesus' thought concerning the Kingdom is in accord on this point with Jewish doctrine; in the same way as, in Pauline theology, the eternal Royalty of Christ begins with the same general judgment.

In Christian doctrine, God will judge—not only according to the principles of Judaism, to compensate for observance of the law, but following more profound reasons which the parables are to reveal to us.

The Workers Hired at the Eleventh Hour

(Matt. 20:1-16)

A scene from peasant life at the time of Jesus. They do not riot, as today, in order to have work. They prefer even not to work. Not much is necessary for living: a piece of bread, a small dried fish.

Morning. The workers are assembled in the market place. The owner of a vineyard comes to hire them. They agree on the salary: a denarius.

At noon the master passes by again. He makes an offer: "I will give you a fair wage." An hour before sunset, some workers are always in the market place: "You go into my vineyard too."

The day ended, they pass by the owner's house in order to receive their pay. The master of the vineyard says to his bailiff: "Call the workers and pay them their wages, starting with the last arrivals and ending with the first."

Those from the eleventh hour went forward and they received a denarius. The first hired went forward expecting to receive more, and they received a denarius. They took their money with a grimace and mumbled against the landowner: "The men who came last have done only one hour, and you have treated them the same as us, though we have done a heavy day's work in all the heat." The landowner summons one of them: "My friends, I am not being unjust to you; did we not agree on one denarius? Take your earnings and go. I choose to pay the

last-comer as much as I pay you. Have I no right
to do what I like with my own? Why be envious
because I am generous?"

Thus, concludes the parable, the last will be first,
and the first, last. This phrase at the end reveals to
us Jesus' intention. There are two classes among
these workers. The workers from the eleventh hour,
contrary to probability, enjoy the landowner's prefer-
ence; that is to say, God's.

The first hired worked twelve hours at a stretch.
But it is not the work that interests the master of the
vineyard, since all, even those who worked only one
hour, receive the same salary. Still, if these last men
had worked better than the others! But the parable
says nothing which might make us suppose this. Its
silence is all the more eloquent in that the Jerusalem
Talmud knows an analogous story, with a point revealing a state of mind completely opposed to that
of Christianity.

"What does the case of Rabbi Boun bar Rabbi
Hijja resemble? That of a king who had engaged many
workers in his service, of which one was more
energetic in his work. Seeing that, what does the
king do? He takes him from the group and walks
with him to and fro. In the evening the workers
arrive to be paid, and he equally pays to the full
the one with whom he walked. Seeing this, his
companions complained, saying: We are fatigued
from working the entire day, and this man who only
exerted himself for two hours receives as much salary

as we? That is because, replied the king, this man here accomplished more in two hours than you in an entire day. Likewise, when Rabbi Boun had studied the law until the age of twenty-eight, he knew it better than a scholar or a pious man would who had studied it until the age of a hundred."

The story was told in this form around the year A.D. 325, in the funeral eulogy for Rabbi Boun. It was a well-known narrative, which could have been known by Jesus. But what a difference in tone! In the Talmud's parable, the salary must be just, and in payment for the work furnished. For the Gospel parable, the exertion is one thing, the pay is another. The landowner does not **have** to be just, according to the jusice we call distributive. The point of the Talmud's parable: one did as much in two hours as in a day; the salary is merited, measured by the quantity of the work furnished. The Gospel parable: the salary is given gratuitously through simple munificence, even to him who worked only one hour, provided he was hired.

For the last comer is hired all the same. The last comer achieves a good end. What is there in his conduct that attracts the master's sympathy to him? For he has sympathy; the master takes up the defense of the situation and of his conduct.

What is there? It is that he has not worked in order to merit his salary, that he was not bothered by this: the master of the vineyard calls him; he, with confidence, hires himself out. He has no other merit.

Let us attentively reread the parable.

The master agrees upon a wage with the first workers. They discussed the conditions. They made an employment contract. Work for one day: a salary of one denarius. The subsequent workers made no contract. The master said: I will give you a just wage. They placed their confidence in him. The eleventh-hour workers neither talked about nor heard talk of a salary: "Go and work in my vineyard." They went. And indeed, they worked with all their heart.

The more one is disinterested in his right, in his salary, the more he is a worker according to God's heart. The eleventh-hour worker was totally disinterested; he gave himself completely. The workers for salary are the Jews of the Pharisaical category. Their life consists in producing works of justice, for which God owes them a heavenly reward. In short God is their debtor.

In the eleventh-hour workers, have we not recognized the heroes of the three great parables on "justice" in Luke? As for the Samaritan, the tax collector, the public sinner, God can exercise his mercy. In return, he contents himself with his creature's confidence. Matthew's parable, indeed, goes further; for "justice by faith" at the last judgment is exalted. It was already the pledge, down here, of the heavenly joy into which God welcomes his good and faithful servants.

Only mercy on the side of God and love on the human side give to the work its religious value. But the work, when it is well done, gives proof of the love from which it proceeds. Whether it constructs temporal houses or heavenly temples, it is necessary, thus, that it be well done, respecting the rules and good architectural traditions. "Order leads to God."

The Crafty Steward (Luke 16:1-9)

Against earthly interests, Christ's revelation opposes the interests of the Kingdom of God. That man put down his temporal cares to "seek the Kingdom and its justice"!

This was already the theme of the brief parables in the Sermon on the Mount. One cannot serve two masters at the same time (Matt. 6:24); it is necessary to choose between the treasure of heaven and that of earth (Matt. 6:19-21). The poor, as if by the natural order of things and making a virtue of necessity, have primordial rights to the Kingdom. The rich are disinherited therein.

Jesus spoke for a society in which wealth and poverty appeared much more stereotyped than in our "developed countries." Poverty remains even today the lot of an immense human population, and the Gospel parables do not reach them. In our "contented" civilization each one among the rich and each one among the poor must fall in line, that all may hear the parable. Each one should listen to the voice that speaks across the depths of his conscience the old words of Jesus, and, momentarily, play the role of "the crafty steward."

However, before reading the parable, it is necessary to rectify an earlier error in the designation of the parable. The title "The Unfaithful Steward" is the most unfaithful to the Master's thought there is, the most "confusing." The first man who put it at the head of the parable adjudged the case from a "casuist" viewpoint. This is what must be avoided. With regard to the handlers of the money, we must take a position of indifference. It little matters that they manage their wealth while observing the rules of human justice, and that they remain "honest." They manage it. And we Christians—who are the "poor" on earth although we possess the Kingdom, that **other** wealth—regard from afar all of this world, which is not ours. Even if we are sociologically "financiers," religiously we are the ones designated the "poor"; and to the degree that we are poor, we keep our distance. We try to imitate Jesus. Someone said to him one day: "Tell my brother to share our inheritance with me." Jesus replied: "Who has established me as the judge of peace, in order to settle your difference [in money matters]?"

A "rich" man does not interest us. A steward of this man, and his account books, and his I.O.U.'s, and his debtors: that does not interest us. What is going to interest us is the cleverness of the steward in his manner of managing money; and we will have to transpose that cleverness to our sphere. (Whether the conduct is honest or deserving of a reprimand does not much matter for us: it is clever.)

"There was a rich man and he had a steward who was denounced to him for being wasteful with his property." This is a common occurrence in the world. Jesus has not to tell us if the accusation is true or false. That is without importance "He called for the man and said, 'What is this I hear about you? Draw me up an account of your stewardship because you are not to be my steward any longer.'" Does the man lack imagination? Is he not rather a victim of his carelessness? His steward alone is capable of examining the accounts. The rich man is content, and he will continue to live on the revenue furnished to him.

"Then the steward said to himself, 'Now that my master is taking the stewardship from me, what am I to do? Dig? I am not strong enough. Go begging? I should be too ashamed. Ah, I know what I will do to make sure that when I am dismissed from office there will be some to welcome me into their homes.'

"Then he called his master's debtors one by one. To the first he said, 'How much do you owe my master?' 'One hundred measures of oil' was the reply. The steward said, 'Here, take your bond; sit down straight away and write fifty.' To another he said, 'And you, sir, how much do you owe?' 'One hundred measures of wheat' was the reply. The steward said, 'Here, take your bond and write eighty.' The master praised the (dishonest) steward for his astuteness."

We must halt. For my part, I do not doubt that Luke copied a text. (Generally he has sources, and he reproduces them docilely. In this parable in particular, indications are not lacking of a style which is not his own.) The basic text said, "The master praised the steward for his astuteness . . ." and saw no difficulty recognizing the cunning of the money handler. Luke changes the situation; as we are thinking, he wishes to stigmatize the conduct of the steward by the addition of the adjective "dishonest." Thus he creates a problem which is not at all in the spirit of the parable, leading us to ask ourselves how one can praise a dishonest employee. A solution for such a problem—it was already, I believe, Luke's—consists in understanding that it is the steward's master who praises: he, at least, does not have to be so particular concerning a question of morality. The basic text remained neutral. It was correct. The only thing Jesus has against money is when it distracts us from the primary attention which we should have for the Kingdom.

Thus, the word of "the Lord"; he explains: "For the children of this world are more astute in dealing with their own kind than are the children of light. And so I tell you this: use money . . . to win you friends . . ."—we return to the neutral source by omitting the words "tainted as it is"—and thus make sure that when it fails you, they will welcome you into the tents of eternity."

Here, Luke strings together a series of authentic words of Jesus, which should destroy the idea that

he could have approved of the attitude, at least
unconstrained, of the steward. "The man who can
be trusted in little things . . ." (this is aimed at the
steward's case, and those of all money handlers) ". . .
can be trusted in great; the man who is dishonest in
little things will be dishonest in great. If then you
cannot be trusted with money [that tainted thing],
who will trust you with genuine riches? And if you
cannot be trusted with what is not yours, who will
give you what is your very own?"

"The Pharisees, who loved money," concludes
Luke, "heard all this and laughed at him. He said to
them, 'You are the very ones who pass yourselves
off as virtuous in people's sight, but God knows your
hearts. For what is thought highly of by men is
loathsome in the sight of God'" (Luke 16:10-15).

The parable of the rich pleasure-seeker and of
poor Lazarus illustrates this last sentence of the
Master. God judges in a different way from men;
his standards are opposed to ours. There will be, in
the other life, a reversal of the situation here below.
God's judgments will be law, and will determine
eternal dispositions.

Jesus related:

"There was a rich man who used to dress in
purple and fine linen and feast magnificently every
day. And at his gate there lay a poor man called
Lazarus, covered with sores, who longed to fill himself with the scraps that fell from the rich man's table.
Dogs even came and licked his sores. Now the poor

man died and was carried away by the angels to
the bosom of Abraham. The rich man also died and
was buried" (Luke 16:19-22).

All ends for the rich man at his beautiful funeral.
He carried away nothing with him. It is the poor
man's turn to be seated at a banquet, that of Abraham, and he has been given the place of honor, "the
bosom of Abraham." Everything changes for the poor
man when he is dead: "In the holy place, Rome hangs
up its tatters." Now it is his turn to receive guests
in the tents of eternity, those who treated him with
consideration in his unhappiness.

Let us learn at the same time to manage money
honestly, and to aid the poor with our resources,
even though modest.

St. Augustine knew some Christians who took the
words of Our Lord literally: "Make friends for yourselves with ill-gotten gain," and he retorted: "Misunderstanding these words, they steal another's property and make use of it in part to give bounty to
the poor; in this way they think to accomplish the
precept. They say: to steal another's property is the
mammon of iniquity; subsequently to give a part of
it, especially to their Christian brothers who are in
need, is to make friends out of the mammon of
iniquity. It is necessary to correct this way of thinking. . . ."

We steal today, but we make use of our larceny
to lead the life of a bad rich man or, rather, simply
of a rich man. In the main, it is better thus than to

come again to Pharisaism by a roundabout going through Christ.

The call of the parables concerning the use of wealth in the face of God's judgment is more real than ever. To give of one's goods for heaven is to introduce the existence of God into our daily life; to affirm, by observing one of Christ's counsels, that God is the living reality which alone merits man's care. In this way man grows by humbling his banal exterior life.

Poverty creates another problem in the modern world. Happily (let us dare to say for logical Christians), because while awaiting a total transformation, as yet problematical, of our civilizations, poverty is one of the most powerful forces of Christian life. Perhaps certain saints have exaggerated, but, shall we say with the poet, "it is good to exaggerate thus." Source of holiness: this refers obviously to true poverty. St. Jerome noted with regard to the **Beati pauperes:** "It is not simple poverty which renders man happy (in the possession of the Kingdom) but poverty because of Christ."

The poor man should remain, in "Christian" society, a consecrated being. Christian civilization of the Middle Ages followed magnificently St. Augustine's principle: the rich have been created for the poor, and the poor have been created for the rich. The poor pray, the rich give, and God magnificently recompenses both of them. May voluntary or accepted poverty remain for a long time to come a test of true Christianity.

VIII

THE COMING IN
GLORY OF JESUS

A hope characterizes Christian eschatology: Jesus will return in glory at the end of time.

"And then," says the Synoptic allegory, "they will see the Son of Man coming in the clouds with great power and glory" (Mark 13:26; Matt. 24.30; Luke 21:27). Primitive Christianity, St. Paul in particular, bears witness to the expectation, sometimes feverish, which stirred up Christ's disciples. "I can see heaven thrown open," Stephen cried out at the moment of his martyrdom, "and the Son of Man standing at the right hand of God" (Acts 7:56). St. Paul taught his Christians "to wait for the Son of God to come from heaven to save us from the retribution which is coming" (1 Thess. 1:10). He described in vivid colors, borrowed from the ceremony of the joyous entry of the sovereigns, the descent of the Lord from heaven, in the glorious apparel of the apocalypse.

This agreement of all of primitive Christianity, this ancientness, the archaic style of expression, would be difficult to explain if Jesus had not himself announced that he "would come upon the clouds." Gospel tradition has, moreover, preserved some of these words, marked with the stamp of authenticity. "I tell you solemnly, there are some of these standing here who will not taste death before they see the Son of Man coming with his kingdom" (Matt. 16:28 and its parallels). "You will see the Son of Man seated at the right hand of the Power and coming on the clouds of heaven" (Matt. 26:64 and its parallels).

These formulas point us toward the seventh chapter of Daniel. The nation of holy ones of the Most High God is there represented by a "Son of Man," who comes on the clouds to receive the Kingdom and the glory from the hands of the judge: "And I saw, coming on the clouds of heaven, one like a son of man . . ." (Dan. 7:13). Judgment is in sight; from the time that Jewish tradition had personalized that enigmatic figure of the "Son of Man," they attributed to him, among the divine attributes, that of judging the living and the dead.

Are we going to be surprised to find again at this moment that influence of the book of Daniel which we noted at the beginning of our study, with respect to the Kingdom of heaven? Our Lord's thought, in order to explain the antithesis which governs the history of the Kingdom, made use of images drawn from the most often read apocalypse in the Palestinian milieu. (The Dead Sea Scrolls borrow from him the term "mystery" in particular.) When the drama of his life led him to foresee, beyond his mortal life, the future outside of time which would be his, was it not completely normal that he continue to express it in the formulas of Daniel's Apocalypse?

The Talents (Matt. 25:14-30; cf. Luke 19:12-27)

"It is like a man on his way abroad who summoned his servants and entrusted his property to them." Thus begins the parable. The situation is that of the Christians after Jesus' death. The absence of all allusion to the resurrection, with the attention uniquely attached to the return of this master, should reveal the prudence of the exegetes. Jesus himself, rather than one or another community leader, exhorts the disciples who, after the death of the "shepherd," will be dispersed like sheep from a flock deprived of its guardian.

The beginning of the parable of the pounds in Luke has colored the story—but the same story—with souvenirs from the Hellenistic kingdoms of the epoch: "A man of noble birth . . ."—a royal prince—". . . went to a distant country . . ."—one thinks of Rome who made and unmade kings—". . . to be appointed king and afterwards return" (Luke 19:12).

Certain details set aside, recent commentators prefer Matthew's version of the parable. We will follow them.

The man on his way abroad summons his servants and entrusts his property to them. It is their task to improve upon it during his absence.

The man is rich, very rich, as befits a prince. To one he gives five talents, to another two, to the last, one, and he departs. The first two servants make the money bear fruit; the last one hid it in the ground. When the master comes back, he demands an accounting. They know his generosity and his severity.

The essential personage of the parable, he who dominates the scene, is the master. He has majesty, absolute sovereign authority without appeal from God. This is also Our Lord, because he left on a long voyage. Act One, during which the wealth is distributed, the master dominates by his generosity and his authority. The Second Act takes place in his absence. But it is an absence which lays stress on the conduct of the servants. Act Three: he reappears. He unites severity with generosity:

We have just alluded to the character of the master: generous, authoritative, severe. The wicked servant perceived among these aspects only his severity: he was a hard man, reaping where he had not sown and gathering where he had not scattered (Matt. 25:24). In other terminology, this is a master whose service is not easy. He strongly resembles the man—and may be the same person—of whom Luke speaks: when the servant returns weary with fatigue after having labored all day long, the master says to him: Prepare supper and serve me first; after which you will eat and drink. He has no sympathetic understanding: when you have done all you have been told to do, say, "We are merely servants: we have done no more than our duty" (Luke 17:7-10).

He is authoritarian and personal. Why does he distribute his wealth with such unrestrained inequality: to one, five talents; to a second, two; and to a third, one? They can well tell us: according to their own capacities. But what does that capacity represent? Only the master is the judge of this, and his criteria remain unknown to us. Moreover, the same master, at the hour for paying his workers, will not take into account the work furnished. He will pay them as he intends: he will pay the same price for a day of harsh labor as for an hour of work.

All that would be nothing. This is a master who appears to be completely disinterested in his servants. He leaves on his trip. The voyage is long, and he is late in coming back. One asks oneself if he will ever return, so long does he linger. He had arranged nothing: no date for his return.

When one serves such a master, the situation is not pleasant. It is agonizing by virtue of this contrast between severity and an apparent withdrawal of authority. Toward this paradoxical situation drawn for us—a master too severe and personal, a master who is disinterested, who is far away—two attitudes are possible.

The wicked servant, humanly, acts with prudence. Of what is he capable? He has been entrusted with a sum of money. He is afraid of losing it, and he hides it as one hides a precious treasure. There is his crime. To hide his master's money is to refuse the risk in making it produce. Now, by its nature, money is productive. In place of giving himself to his task without reflecting, the servant thinks to shelter his situation from possible jolts. The treasure hidden in the ground—he thinks no more about it. He can no longer think about it. And he has time for himself. He has dodged the complete service which the master demanded, which God demands. He had a bad calculation. On the other hand, the good servants understand the situation, are confident, and work.

Some commentators are in danger of committing the fault of the bad servant, when they imagine that the talents of the parable are the natural qualities of the body or the soul, which God must use to advantage. That exegesis, of a Pelagian sort, was so common that it contributed to the formation of the French language; the word "talent," with its sense of aptitude, capacity, competency given by nature or acquired through work, undergoes the influence of this parable through the shift of a metaphor: "If your body is a precious talent which should improve in the hands of God, put it early into business and do not wait to give it to him when he may be on the point of burying it in the ground" (Boussuet).

That exegesis corresponds admirably to the tendency of our age. One gives oneself to humanity with all one's natural talents. Holiness is free expansion, love, and joy. **The Spiritual Life,** in 1946, dedicated a special issue to the question: "Toward what type of holiness are we going?" Father Plé sums up the investigation: "To judge after the collection of replies what, in our days, one expects from holiness is the exaltation of man: the saint is an accomplished man, a human success. Holiness is the presence of God in the man, in whom all the riches find themselves neither diminshed nor sacrificed, but perfect and surpassed."

God does not read inquiries, for he continues to make his saints as he sees fit. One cannot love them all, like that lady member of the Young Catholic Workers who did not approve of St. John of the Cross "because he has an unhuman holiness" which "seems to go against the parable of the talents." (Happily, there are still Christians for whom St. John of the Cross is a preferred saint: such as the officer, a former leader of the underground who, on the same subject, believes total privation to be absolutely necessary, the "nothing, nothing, nothing" upon which reposes his entire doctrine, "most particularly in our era where intemperance in all matters, as much on the material plane as on the spiritual plane, deprives man of that important solitude, that interior and exterior silence necessary for the normal penetration of the Holy Spirit. In particular on the intellectual plane and in the domain of education, the abuse of learning enervates spirits.")

The sense of the parable is, however, very clear. The master shares his own goods among his servants. What would these be if not spiritual goods? The Fathers are unanimous. Christ calls his servants, that is to say for example, those whom he crowns with the honor of the priesthood; he gives spiritual graces according to the disposition and the capacity of each one (Cyril of Alexandria). For St. Hilary and for St. Jerome the parable speaks of the preaching of the gospel. The enormity of the sum which the master confides to these people, who have never had in their belts more than a few small coins, proves, if there could be any need of proof, that it is a question of a completely different kind of money.

Still, a problem is inserted into the parable: the master distributed his goods according to the, at least presumed, capacity of his servants. A preliminary remark which explains much: this problem never preoccupied the saints. Neither St. Paul, the theorist of the cross, who utilizes to the utmost, while protesting that they are useless, his gifts as a thinker, a man of action, an orator, and a writer. Nor St. Augustine, who preaches to his provincials at Hippo in the finest literary language. Nor St. Francis of Assisi; yet what he spent of Italian ingenuity, poetic and human, in the service of his Lord!

Without scruple and without thinking about it, the saints dispense their natural talents; for their attention is fixed upon God. Their intelligence and their faculties for action are like channels through which God's gifts flow; the source is God; the human faculties, the natural talents let water pass from the source without carrying it off for themselves, without knowing even that the water is passing. What is important is that the gifts of God are poured out upon the world.

Often they gained that victory of grace over their human activities by great struggle. In the process of their conversion, they one day shattered their natural talents at the foot of the crucifix. And then, those talents were returned to them. But they no longer belong to them. They are lent. They are truly the talents of the parable.

The good servants, consumed by confidence in the master, throw themselves headlong into God's work, turned toward the ideal which they glimpse.

We do not know precisely what our master exacts from us, if it is not that he will never be satisfied until the day when he will return. In the Old Testament the task was fixed. One knew the days on which to abstain from work (the Sabbath and the neomenias), the days of fasting. One knew which animals one could eat, and those from which it was necessary to abstain. One knew the sacrifices to offer: the occasion for a holocaust, for a peace offering, for a red cow. The task could be complicated. It was clearly fixed; one knew what to do. One did not have to go beyond it. In the New Testament we no longer know what to do. The good-servant types are the saints: these are inimitable. How do you wish to serve when you have before you not only a canonized saint but a simple candidate like Charles de Foucauld. Struck by a word from the abbot Huvelin: "Our Lord has so completely taken the last place that no one could ever rob him of it . . . ," he earnestly desires not the last place, since it is taken, but the next to last one. He will become a Trappist, in a distant monastery, Abkès in Syria, to be more forgotten, poorer, closer to the land where Jesus suffered and worked, where he can bury himself always more in abjection; these are his own terms. And never will he feel sufficiently buried, even to the day in which he finishes his harsh existence, "assassinated by those men for whom he prayed so much, walked so much over sand and rock, suffered so much from thirst and heat, studied so many days and nights, accepted so much loneliness, so greatly pained in body and spirit."

For the former French officer, the parable was accomplished. Finally it was Jesus' turn to speak: "Well done, good and faithful servant. Because you have been faithful in a few things, I will make you master over many. Enter into the joy of your Lord."

The Ten Virgins (Matt. 25:1-12)

The Kingdom of God will also be like ten virgins invited to be in a wedding procession; they must carry their lamps, for the procession will be made at night. They wait in the bride's house. The bride-groom is coming to take her, to conduct her to his own home where the wedding feast will take place.

In the parable of the talents we dealt with a severe master, who exacted much work. Here it is a wedding, the celebration **par excellence** in a Galilean village. The joy denotes the straining of our Christian life toward the coming of Christ in glory. Heaven and earth are reunited; like a luminous cloud, glory hangs over our earthly existence. We see in faith the heavenly Jerusalem toward which we march.

But among the ten virgins there are five sensible ones and five foolish and improvident ones. These latter are concerned with their attire, with combing their tresses and perfuming themselves; they have not forgotten their lamps, traditional for the wedding; they carry them with elegance. But they have not considered the prudence of taking a provision of oil. The sensible virgins, along with their lamps, take oil in their flasks.

All keep watch, awaiting the bridegroom. And because he is late, they grow drowsy and fall asleep. The sleep of the wise virgins is light. They dream of hearing the signal. They are ready. The others sleep a deep sleep. Do they know yet why they are there?

Someone goes out and hears the clamor of the joyous troop in the distance: "The bridegroom is here! Go out and meet him."

At this moment the foolish virgins revive themselves. They panic: "Give us some of your oil: our lamps are going out." Unhappily it is a characteristic of the prudent ones to lack a certain facile generosity. Consider the ant of the fable teller. "You had better go to those who sell it and buy some for yourselves." The imprudent ones will miss the arrival of the bridegroom. The procession has gone; already the lamps are shining with all their brilliance in the wedding hall. The foolish have spoiled their joy. They have spoiled everything, for the bridegroom reveals his identity when they knock at the closed door: "I tell you solemnly, I do not know you." The master in the parable of the talents, hard and severe in his justice, reappears.

For not having taken an elementary precaution,

the virgins miss the call. They had thought only of their feminine frivolities from the moment of the invitation. If, through a well-understandable politeness, the liturgy reserves for "Christian virgins" (the wise) a privileged application of the parable (since the Gelasian Sacramentary: "because they await, it is said of them, the heavenly bridegroom, their lamps lighted, provided with oil for the waiting period"), in reality we are all summoned in his script. We are told at our baptism, when we are presented with a candle: "Receive this burning light, and keep the grace of your baptism throughout a blameless life. Observe the commandments of God, and then when the Lord comes to his heavenly wedding feast, you may be able to meet him with all the saints in the halls of heaven, and live forever and ever. Amen."

In the Eastern liturgies, where the old traditions are faithfully preserved, and where one looks upon the Mass as a prelude to the coming of the Lord, the faithful beseech God: "Prepare us also, in order that having remained innocent, our lamps lighted, we may go forward to the encounter with your only Son." They commemorate the dead "who are invited to the wedding and ardently await the heavenly bridegroom."

The Fathers are not deficient in the use of this beautiful theme in their exhortations to the faithful. "Today we are in pain," cried out St. Augustine, "and the flame of our lamps wavers under the influence and temptations of this century; but may it always burn stronger and more ardently, and may the wind of temptation brighten rather than extinguish its fire."

Perhaps we find all of that very anachronistic. In effect, there are not many themes which appear of less importance in Christianity than that of the return of Christ. But it was so almost from the beginning of the Church. Sections of the parable recall that the bridegroom is late in coming, and that the virgins fall asleep. These are surely the sections which tradition took care to state precisely, in the face of the situation in the second Christian generation which was impatient at the delay.

St. Paul waited, hesitated, worked. "Our salvation is even nearer than it was when we were converted," he wrote to the Romans (13:11). At the same time, he put the Thessalonians on guard against an impatience which would have taken away their taste for work. His idea was that it was necessary to expedite the current affairs of this world, while waiting for the other world. Later, he thrilled with joy at the thought of his death, the next encounter with his Lord—before His return.

Father Teilhard de Chardin, who was preoccupied after his own fashion, but more than anyone, with the end of the world, or rather with the birth of the New Earth—which is not quite the same thing—wrote a page concerning the wait for "the consummation of the divine milieu": "On the hour and the modalities of that formidable occurrence, it would be vain, the Gospel makes us aware, to speculate. But we must **wait** for it. . . . Historically, the waiting has never ceased to guide, like a torch, the progress of our Faith. . . . Alas, a slightly infantile haste, joined to an error in perspective, which made the first Christian generation believe in the imminent return of Christ, has left us deceived and rendered us suspicious. The World's resistance to Good has come to disconcert our faith in the Reign of God. A certain pessimism, perhaps sustained by an exaggerated conception of the original fall, has brought us to believe that the World is decidedly bad and incurable. . . . So, we have left the fire in our sleeping hearts dim. Without doubt, with greater or less anguish, we see individual death approaching. Without doubt, still, we pray and we act conscientiously, 'that God's Reign may come.' But, in truth, how many are there among us who really thrill, in the bottom of their hearts, at the foolish hope of a refounding of **our** Earth? . . . Of what sort is the Christian in whom the impatient nostalgia for Christ succeeds, not even to submerge (as would be necessary) but only to balance, the cares of love or of human interests?"

Is the theology of history contained in the treasure of the parables? The actual movement of the world is surely neither rectilinear, nor always in the direction of spiritual values, and these concern us before all else: "When the Son of Man returns, will he find faith on earth?" This is an exhortation to ceaselessly enliven our faith, by an intense love for Christ and for the Truth. This love of truth, in which is included the world's progress, suffices to restore to our faith and our hope all their enthusiasm.

Because of the great Christian hope, and to the extent that it is taken seriously, life resembles an exile. The virgins heard the cry in the night: "The bridegroom is here! Go out and meet him." The theme is old in the world. It has been restored to a place of honor by contemporary biblical and liturgical literature, sometimes under the form of the exodus, sometimes under that of the Passover.

In the Septuagint version of Genesis 14:13, Abraham "the Hebrew" was first translated as Abraham "the emigrant." Abraham, the father of believers, of Christians, of the new race, is essentially a voyager, a pilgrim, an emigrant, he who leaves his home: "Leave your country, your family and your father's house, for the land I will show you. . . . All the tribes of the earth shall bless themselves by you" (Gen. 12:1-3.) To leave his country, to renounce the traditions of his race, the sweetness of the ancestral hearth, to travel, to pitch his tent at Bethel, to depart, to camp in the desert, to descend into Egypt, to return to Canaan: such is the life of Abraham, the perpetual traveler, the emigrant.

Abraham is the image of those who leave their home in order to enrich themselves spiritually. Philo of Alexandria entitled one of his treatises **On the Migration of Abraham.** He begins with the text, "Leave your country, . . . " which he interprets "to put aside the body, sensation, reasoning"; he teaches that the Hebrews are the race which passes from perceptible things to spiritual things; that there is a book in the Bible entitled Exodus, the Departure; that the

Passover signifies passage, etc. The Jewish philosopher is still nostalgic for the nomadic life.

The theme reappears in the Epistle to the Hebrews: "It was by faith that Abraham obeyed the call to set out for a country that was the inheritance given to him and his descendants, and that he set out without knowing where he was going. By faith he arrived, as a foreigner, in the Promised Land, and lived there as if in a strange country, with Isaac and Jacob, who were heirs with him of the same promise. They lived there in tents while he looked forward to a city founded, designed and built by God" (Heb. 11:8-10). This is why St. Peter exhorts us: "I urge you, my dear people, while you are visitors and pilgrims, to keep yourselves free from the selfish passions that attack the soul" (1 Pet. 2:11).

"My brothers," cried Clement Romain, abandoning the foreign land of this earth, "do the will of him who has called us and fear not to leave this world. . . . And know, brethren, that our exile in this world of the flesh is short, that the promise of Christ is great and admirable, that this is the repose of the future kingdom and of eternal life. What will we do to attain it, if it is not to live in holiness and justice, and to esteem this world as a stranger, and to not desire the things of this world? No one can serve two masters at the same time."

These formulas were not conventional at that time. The Christians' city was being built in heaven; in the earthly city they were the banished, the outlaws. Thus they were, whether one will or not, a race of heroes, of apostles, of martyrs. "Anyone who does not carry his cross and come after me cannot be my disciple" (Luke 14:27). It was a question, there-fore, to make of one's Christian life a fortress, not a pleasure villa.

St. Basil wrote to the prefect of the emperor Valentius: "Confiscation cannot touch him who has nothing. . . . neither (can) exile alarm him who be-longs to no place and who considers himself every-where on earth as a pilgrim; nor torture nor death terrify him who is impatient to go to God."

When monks and cenobites peopled the desert, we do not know if they fled before persecution, or if they were impassioned by solitude. Later, the ideal did not cease its hold on Christians. Being no longer obligatory pilgrims, some saints did it by free choice. All of Christianity at that time moved toward the holy places: Rome, St. James of Compos-tella, Jerusalem. It is not without emotion that one discovers at the foot of the Alps or of the Pyrenees these pilgrim refuges of which the chapel is always venerated by the shepherds and the peasants. How many good Christians, during that epoch, consecrated themselves to the pilgrim state and found holiness in it, since St. Alexis, St. Roch. Nearer to us, one of the last, St. Benedict Labre.

There is in pilgrimage, in the hermitage, a "conse-cration" to poverty, to the total abandonment of country, of family, of comforts, sometimes of seemli-

ness, which puts the body and the soul in a state
of self-abnegation, of perpetual departure from self.
The true pilgrim looks for Jesus and finds him. One
goes into the distance, the most distant possible, for
paradise is even further yet. "Their soul, to those
people, is in no wise similar to that of others. They
are those who march, who wish to die for their idea.
How could they resemble the others, those who
remain in place, enclosed in monotonous and barren
dreaming?"

I see again the fresco in St. Mark's Hospital in
Florence; on a tympanum of a door: the two pilgrims
on the road to Emmaus. Christ is with them; he also
is dressed like a pilgrim, with a traveler's tunic, staff,
medals around his neck. The two pilgrims raise
bewildered eyes toward him, in which is mirrored
the new world.

EPILOGUE

At the moment that his disciples begin to penetrate the sense of the parables, Jesus declares to them: "Well then, every scribe who becomes a disciple of the kingdom of heaven is like a householder who brings out from his storeroom things both new and old" (Matt. 13:52). Every disciple, every Christian is aimed at, but especially he who is in charge of teaching.

The householder has squeezed into his coffers and his closets the rich family apparel and some new garments, running the gamut of precious materials; he makes use of them according to the circumstances. In this manner Christians possess the parables in their treasuries today. New things, for they are the teaching of the Master who did not wish to sew new material onto an old garment; old things, for if he renewed all the law, he did not change it essentially, and every Christian respects in it the will of God. Garments as old as the prophecies of the Old Testament; for Jesus inherited from the prophets the images with which he dressed his thought in order to manifest eternal secrets, all the while veiling the brilliance of the light.

True treasures: the parables contain the Kingdom of heaven.

We have taken seriously the words which Jesus addressed to the Twelve: "To you it is given to know the secrets of the kingdom of heaven." While speaking in parables he was conscious of constructing a spiritual world as yet unknown. The prophecies were realized; the things hidden since the creation of the world were unveiled (Matt. 13:35). At first it was the unimaginable manner in which God founded his Kingdom, upon a Word come from heaven and accepted in the secret of the heart, with the contrast between the humility of the beginning and the magnificence of the future. It was, in the next place, the transformation of "religion" through the revelation of "mercy," from which was going to be born a proportionate "justice." All that would have as a consequence the rehabilitation of men scorned by the religious leaders of Judaism and the transference of the privileges of the Chosen People to a people who will bear the fruits of the Kingdom.

Some parables are consecrated to the break of Jesus and his embryonic community with Judaism. Henceforth Jesus' thought is going to consider more expressly the future reserved to his work. A new society succeeds the former religious society. Without ceasing to be a chosen people, the Church presents itself to the world as the sign of the change in the divine plan.

The diverse parables of the planting already permit us to glimpse, between the seeding of the Kingdom and the eschatological harvest, a growth period of indeterminate duration; it is up to God to determine the moment when the harvest will be ripe. The idea is stated more precisely in the parables of the feast and of the husbandmen. The first ones invited to the messianic feast refused the honor; in their place, last-minute guests, recruited from everywhere, even from paganism, enjoy the wealth of the Kingdom of God. The feast endures a thousand years, according to the calculations of Judaism. Under another image, the peasants to whom the master of the vineyard had confided the Kingdom did not render to him the fruits which he expected; they will be punished, the vineyard will be taken back from them and given to "others." After a logion of archaic coinage, these others constitute a "people." An earthly period opens. God alone knows its duration.

Jesus is not without knowing what will be his own destiny in the drama which pounces upon Judaism. He will share in John the Baptist's lot, that of the prophets, that of all the just, and his community itself will be carried away by the storm. However, a rainbow dominates the tempest. At the decisive moment, God will make the Son of man appear upon the clouds of heaven, he who is the representative of the people of the saints of the Most High God; and he will restore to him the Kingdom, the empire of the world, and all his glory. Jesus condensed the great hope in the solemn affirmation retained by tradition: "the Son of Man will come upon the clouds!"

The prophecies and apocalyptic references of Jesus will aid apostolic men to steer the bark of the Church through tempests: Christian equilibrium will establish itself upon the traditions of the Lord. When, at the very beginning, the waiting made it too anxious and restless, the apostles, Paul in particular, calmed it by leaning it "on the word of the Lord" (1 Thess. 4:15). Later, confronted by the slowness of the parousia, they revived the wait for the day when Christ would give the crown of glory "to all those who love his coming." "Keep watch and pray," they repeated, "for you know not at what hour the Lord will come."

Is it not still fidelity to Jesus' words, guarded and explained by tradition, which, across all the vicissitudes of a Church tossed between persecutions and spiritual graces, will save Christians from illusions and disillusions? The Church knows itself to be a stranger in the world. She knows also that she is the light of the same world and the salt of the earth. Nothing can surprise her or confuse her in her faith and her hope.

As the mother's breast awaits the birth of the child, the Church nourishes souls and prepares them for the true life, that which will begin in eternity. Guardian of the teachings of Jesus, she is the solid terrain on which repose our ephemeral lives.

Jesus ended the Sermon on the Mount with a parable:

"Therefore, everyone who listens to these words of mine and acts on them will be like a sensible man who built his house on rock. Rain came down, floods rose, gales blew and hurled themselves against that house, and it did not fall: it was founded on rock. But everyone who listens to these words of mine and does not act on them will be like a stupid man who built his house on sand. Rain came down, floods rose, gales blew and struck that house, and it fell; and what a fall it had!" (Matt. 7:24-27).

One still perceives, across these strophes, the unleashing of Palestinian storms, the noise of the torrents of water and the fracas of the collapsed houses. It is up to us to build our houses—the hurricanes of this world being what they are—upon unshakable rock.